Forward Press Poets 2009

The Midlands

Edited by Forward Press Editors

First published in Great Britain in 2009 by:
Forward Press
Remus House
Coltsfoot Drive
Peterborough
PE2 9JX
Telephone: 01733 890099
Website: www.forwardpress.co.uk

Book Design by Samantha Wood & Tim Christian

SB ISBN 978-1-84418-513-9

Foreword

Here at Forward Press our aim has always been to provide a bridge to publication for as many undiscovered poets as possible. We firmly believe that poetry should be accessible to all and most importantly should connect with the reader. Over the past 21 years we have published a hugely diverse range of poems from writers young and old, creating anthologies that celebrate the wealth of writing talent on offer. With the inclusion of both traditional rhymes and more modern verse, there is always something to suit everyone's tastes.

This latest collection of poems written with creative flair and a passion for the local area is sure to engage and entertain. We hope you agree that Forward Press Poets 2009 - The Midlands is one to treasure and return to time and again. .

Contents

Tom Ritchie....1
Padi Vincent....2
Wendy Deaves....3
Rachel Green....4
Celia Cooper....4
F G Challenger....5
Joyce Dunkley....5
John William Bowen....6
Derrick Wooding....7
Peter Barnes....8
Marilyn K Hambly....9
Anne Palmer....10
Rita Dilks....11
Dorothy Jean Stirland....12
Zena Foster....13
Jonathan Gilbert....14
Doris May Hyde....14
Kathleen Egan....15
Ivan Langham....15
C Greed....16
Joanne Hattershun....17
Linda Knight....18
David Robinson....19
Pamela Sanders....20
Rita Wilde....21
Lois Burton....22
Brenda Reville....23
Richard Cluroe....23
Hazel Palmer....24
Ian Cresswell....25
Freda Straw....26
Annamarie Yates....27
Barbara Fletcher....28
Gillian Beardow....28
Ronald Martin....29
Gavin Cooke....29
Susie Crozier....30
Mark Marsden....31
Margaret Edge....32
Simone Summerscales....32
Steven Michael Pape....33
Brian Large....33
John Franks....34
W Currie....35
Rachel Sidebottom....36
Dulcie E Walker Miranda....36
Deb Thurland....37
Ella Wright....37
Anne Bailey....38
Pat Langton....40
Hazel Deathridge....41
Sheila Harris....42
Richard F Magan....43
Jane Walker-Okeover....44
Bette Walklate....46
Carl Carter....47
Bernie Adams....48
Hilary J Cairns....48
Joy Wright....49
Derek Oakley....49
Andrew Watts....50
Tracey Jane Taylor....51
Vivienne Brocklehurst....52
Dee Degnan....53
Vivien Steels....54
Samantha Rose....55
Suzette Virginia Floyed....56
Iris Burgess....57
Michael Cotton....58
Mary Pauline Winter, nee: Coleman....59
E Riggott....60
Mary Shepherd....60
S K Singleton....61
Susanne Humphries....61
Jan Lovell....62
Sandra Bentley....63
Anne Sackey....64
Janet Starkey....65
Trevor Foster....66
Shirley Mather....67
Tracey Kesterton....68
Lydia Barnett....69
Ada Pain....70
Joan Gray....71
Alan Hattersley....71
Desmond Chapman....72
Myrtle Lucas....72
Nicola Buxton....73
John Younger....73
James Stephen Thompson....74
John Waby....75
N Bates....76

George Nicklin....77
Madge Gilbey....78
Judith Mary Drinkhill....79
Robert Walker....79
Corinne Ashton....80
Jean Dickens....80
Richard Napierski....81
Rosie Hues....82
Vann Scytere....83
Elizabeth Timmins....84
Lilian Bullock....85
Wayne Fisher....86
Linda Jennings....88
John Slim....89
Dorina Shannon....90
Pat Evans....91
Arnold Wesker....92
Carol Bradford....93
David Walter....94
Nigel Pearce....95
Mark Walker....96
Graham Saxby....97
Paul Byron Norris....98
June Picken....98
Freda Terry....99
Peter Maher....100
Gemma Smith....101
Rhowen-Margot Brown....102
H Griffiths....103
Lorraine Bosworth....104
Eileen Nancy Blackmore....105
Carol Bartram....106
Elizabeth Corr....107
Liz Cameron....107
Jeff Hobson....108
Anthony Hull....109
Iris Covell....110
Ted Hancock....111
Percy Walton....112
Vera May Waterworth....112
Betty Maureen Rollitt....113
Marguerite Kendrick....113
Janet Emery....114
Irene Grace Corbett....115
John Keyse....116
Ann Keenleyside....117
Hazel McMullan....118
Lorraine Haslam....119
Alison Hodge....120
Christine M Powell....121
R O'Shaughnessy....122
Paul Thompson....123
Peter Wallace....124
Roderick Scorgie....125
Robert Fallon....126
Tina Hall....126
Pauline Christina Knight....127
Mary Wain....127
B Reeve....128
Edmund St George Mooney....129
Christine Hawthorne....130
Betty Hattersley....131
Frances Marie Cecelia Harvey....132
Derrick Bright....132
Kenneth Berry....133
Fliss Edwards....134
Brenda Dove....135
Leslie Salmen....136
Janet Hughes....136
Carole Payne....137
Carl Kemper....138
Shirley Roberts....139
Joan Moore....140
Sylvia Betts....141
Linda Ann Marriott....142
Patricia Lee....142
Jan Wilson....143
Eileen Robinson....143
Kathleen Bartholomew....144
Josephine Riley....144
Maureen Barnett....145
Ann Humphrey....145
Sandra Minnikin....146
Jacqui Page....147
Marie Haswell....148
Elizabeth Morris....149
Edith Mee....150
Rex Duncan....151
Bakewell Burt....152
Janet Hannan....153
E Catherine Gray....154
John Hewing....155
Richard Hackney....156
Julia White....157
R L Cooper....158
Paul Gamble....159
Pamela Green....160
Deana Constable....162
Don Goodwin....162
Patricia Anne Withnall....163

Jean Cullop ... 164
Marlene Doy ... 165
Lisa Pease ... 165
Catherine M Armstrong ... 166
Andy Jenkinson ... 167
John Pierrepont ... 168
N J Brocks ... 169
Pat Dring ... 170
Sharon Reed ... 171
Roy PJ Mullin ... 172
Stan Solomons ... 173
Julia Richdale Ellis ... 173
Colin Hinds ... 174
Sadie Brown ... 174
Jessie Smith ... 175
Brenda M Hadley ... 176
Denise Angood ... 177
Christina Burnell ... 178
Stan Coombs ... 179
Melvin Dean ... 179
Colin Griffiths ... 180
Anthony Newton ... 181
Sheila Ellen Wright ... 182
Pauline Vinters ... 183
Sharon Lambley ... 184
Jenny Amery ... 185
Peter Godfrey ... 186
Joan Elizabeth Blissett ... 187
Rosemary Eades ... 188
Stephanie Lynn Teasdale ... 189
Sheila Sharpe ... 190
Sandra Elliker ... 191
Cecelia Cran ... 192
Juliet C Eaton ... 193
Gordon Dangerfield ... 194
Jessica Heafield ... 194
Elizabeth Stockley ... 195
Tom Hanson ... 196
Roy Taylor ... 197
Jane Day ... 198
Errol Kavan ... 199
Teresa Billington ... 200
Janet Brown ... 200
Richard Michael Grew ... 201
Tyrone Dalby ... 202
Rosie Oakes ... 204
Nigel Lloyd Maltby ... 205
J Hillas ... 206
David Peniston-Bird ... 206
Gwendoline Bennett ... 207
Diane Young ... 207
Margaret Siddans ... 208
Lucy Green ... 209
Maggie Camps ... 210
Pauline Hill ... 211
Eileen Henderson ... 212
Jean Dutfield ... 212
Richard Chapman ... 213
Michael Spittles ... 213
Doreen Sylvester ... 214
Stephen Green ... 214
James Stephen Cameron ... 215
Paula Johnson ... 216
Pat Hunter ... 217
Isobel Cosford ... 218
Maddy Scott ... 219
Gregory Whitehead ... 220
Peter Terence Ridgway ... 221
Claire Walsh ... 222
Elizabeth Hayden-Jones ... 223
Paul Williams ... 224
Natasha Watkins ... 224
John Pegg ... 225
Julia Pegg ... 226
Clare Milsom ... 227
Frank Baggaley ... 228
Sue Herschell ... 228
Sheila Richardson ... 229
Jean Bailey ... 229
B Baxter ... 230
Lisa Quinn ... 230
Cas Lake ... 231
Ben Macnair ... 232
Terence Powell ... 233
David Denny ... 234
John A Turner ... 235
Owen Davies ... 236
Paul Holland ... 237
Angela Allen ... 238
Margaret Goldstraw ... 239
J Card ... 240
Maureen Butcher ... 242
Richard Vernon ... 242
L G Thomas ... 243
Mandy Barrow ... 244
Mary Lefebvre ... 245
Lydia Talbot ... 246
A Woolley ... 247
Marilyn Gunn ... 248
Keith Forrest ... 249

Deborah Harvey 250
Ronald Astbury 251
Norman Plant 252
Lady Sandie Smith 252
V J Cleaver 253
John Winston-Smith 253
Ian Proctor 254
Christopher Mills 254
Walter Mottram 255
Rachel Hall-Smith 256
Maureen Baxter 257
Clive Hughes 258
Audrey Faulkner 259
Patrick Fitzhenry 260
Barbara Young 261
Audrey Faulkner O'Connor 262
Rita Hardiman 263
Jonathan Simms 264
Patricia Jeanne Hale 264
Mavis Newell 265
Barry Powell 266
Lucy Williams 267
Charmian Howell 268
Irene Hinton 268
Pamela Reynolds 269
Richard Charles 269
Joy Grant 270
Christopher Higgins 271
Jean Elizabeth Lewis 272
Frances Neale 272
R I G Doody 273
Heida 274
TB Rees 275
Frances Taylor 276
Jackie Davies 277
Steve Allen 277
John Daniel Rosser 278
Kerri Moore 279
Hilarie Grinnell 280
George Cowley 280
Denise Edmonds 281
Ralph Watkins 282
Roger Mosedale 282
Mike Storer 283
Irene Barton 283
Lisa Burton 284
Darren P Morrall 285
Marie Francis 286
Samantha Williams 287
Leslie Frank Checkley 288
Lynda Ann Green 289
Christina Fowler 290
W Stevens 291
Jacqueline Claire Davies 291
Cedric Thrupp 292
Brian Harris 292
William Shire 293
Janet Harmer 293
Kate Arkell 294
Doreen Gardner 294
Pam Jeames 295
Kim Gourlay Almey 296
Gary Lanham 297
Brian Bates 297
Carrie Summers 298
Matthew Thomas 299
Angela Cutrale Matheson 299
Joan Winwood 300
Ruth Warrington 300
Josephine Sylvia Huckvale 301
Naomi Portman 301
Jane McGloin 302
Elizabeth Lee 303
N Stokes 303
Anita Quin 304
M V Bayes 305
Adrianne Jones 306
Carole Pearson 307
Michelle Barnes 308
David M Walford 308
Florence Barnard 309
Joan Hosker 310
David Daymond 311
Anne Williams 312
Bushra Latif 312
Mary Farrelly 313
Constance Finn 313
Merle Sadler 314
Oliver Carlin 314
David Sawyer 315
Sana Arshad 315
Gwen Jones 316
George White 316
Barbara Parker 317
Sheila Hodgkins 317
Sheila Bates 318
Brenda Brownhill 319
Eric Wilks 320
Osgood Browne 321
Jacqui Boote 322

Margaret Jones 322
R L Bennett 323
Priya-Jasmine Sangha 324
Eileen Bales 325
Trevor Wiggan 326
Heather Lynes-King 327
David Donaldson 328
Betty Tordoff 329
Philip Sanders 330
Peter Corne 330
G White 331
Margaret Ashfield 331
Christine Preece 332
A Rice 332
Jeanette Middleton 333
Graham Griffiths 333
Ron Smith 334
John Burman 335
J Wicks 336
Christopher Rothery 337
June Sedgebear 338
Kerry Lovatt 339
Michael Thomas Hill 340
J Brown 340
Marilyn Simper 341
Dave K Whalley 342
Joan Hawkes 343
Judy Barklam 343
Tracey Skivington 344
Mark L Hewitt 345
Grace Anderson 346
Zoe French 346

The Poems

This Is The Day - That Special Day

This is the day - that special day
A day you will recall;
The day you'll give your child away
And this before us all;
Who gives this bride, I asked of you,
No hesitation thee,
When you replied with the words I do,
Your presentation free;
So why the clown - just like a goose?
Where beautiful the bride
You must sit down - you've no excuse,
There dutiful beside.

Now all of you, who're gathered here
Must fully understand,
Where once a rose - your heart's a tear,
A tear should keep in hand;
What e'er the cause you feel this way,
Think ne'er the years gone by,
The courage you must show today,
You know the reasons why.
So father take your daughter's cue
And let go while you can,
There's no one here a fool of you,
Disposed to call a ban.

You've other children here as well,
Older wed than she,
So many tears - I cannot tell,
Much more than any sea;
But this one's cut you to the quick,
Her handsome groom nearby,
She's chosen him - love's awesome trick,
No room the inner sigh . . .
So take your seat, proud father dear,
Ne'er vain your daughter brave;
There's no defeat, her beauty fair,
Refrain! - You're but her slave!

Tom Ritchie

Pause For Reflection

I look in the mirror and for Heaven's sake,
think someone's made a dreadful mistake,
cos I'm your galloping gran.
Not too thin,
nor too fat.
(but sometimes,
I will wear a hat.)
cos I'm a gran,
a super,
dooper,
not a party-pooper,
just a gorgeous, glamorous, galloping gran -
now fancy that!

I do all the things that grandmothers oughter,
lend my jeans to my favourite granddaughter,
I'm not too fat,
not too thin,
have a well-hydrated,
firmed up skin
and I gave you the gift of laughter.

You can see it in my eyes,
my smiling eyes,
my hair all spiked,
silver and shining,
dragon tattoo, with its moon aligning
and boots right up to my thighs,
that I'm your gran,
your present-day gran,
tattooed, trendy and slim,
almost always in disguise.

I'm a party gran,
a hearty gran,
a gran who's a right good mover,
(though I must admit,
when I've done my bit,
it'll take me three days to recover.)

I'm a frisky gran,
a whisky gran
and when I feel like a bit of a jig,

I know you will join me
and dance like on holiday
and both of us not care a fig.

Though I'm a small size gran,
I'm a street-wise gran
who can pack a verbal punch;
you I'll defend
right up to the end,
against any who threaten your bunch.

Cos I'm a listening gran
a hearing gran,
but never anyone's fool,
don't lie to me or be snide to me
or even think of
bunking off school.

For I am a galloping gran,
a gran cool,
steadfast and true
and as I glance in this glance
I think of you lass.

On reflection, am I seeing you?

Padi Vincent

21

21 years, well really!
You have done so much for the community
Giving people a chance
To put words on paper, what a glance,
Making us feel we can use our output,
These words, one word means so much,
21 years - a year to remember.
From all of the months, obviously in September.
So thank you for being a friend of ours
And helping us to build our towers
Of hope.

Wendy Deaves

Thistledown

on the canicular breeze
a thistle seed blows
in Brownian motion
brushing the ground
before flying high above the rooftops
'fairy horses' we called them
when I was a child -
catch them to make a wish
and for a moment I am tempted
to leave my keyboard and books and brushes
and go racing
barefoot into the meadow

Rachel Green

Death Of A Tree

There you lie, recumbent
On the back of a lorry
People who had once gazed at your beauty
Hardly notice you're passing by . . .

Your branches shorn off
By men, eager to get to your wood . . .

Perhaps in a little while
People will once again admire you
But in a different shape . . .

But for the living tree
It is the end . . .

Celia Cooper

The Open Gate

Life, the ever open gate.
A chance, hope of getting by.
Some place to pause in times of doubt.
To give one time to think things out.

It beckons us to wander through.
In meadows green and pastures new.
Where we could stroll with someone dear.
Alas, maybe, no longer here.

A gap you think as at the gate.
Think on, do not commiserate.
An open gate, an open mind.
Life's like that, it can be kind.

So wander through, stretch out your stride.
Through that gate is your other side.
Your absent ones gave you that space.
So walk with God, with hope, and grace.

F G Challenger

The Estate

My heart aches for the meadows
That I knew when I was young,
Those cool, green, pleasant acres
I used to walk among.
I knew each tree, each bush that grew
And where the blackbird nested
I knew the bank where rabbits played
And where the grass snake rested.
Alas! those days have passed away
And where the rabbits played
Are houses, shops and pavements grey
Which hands of men have made.
But my heart aches for the meadows
That I knew when I was young.

Joyce Dunkley

Trees

Mighty Oak why do you take so long to grow?
It's something I long to know
Two hundred years, maybe more
Cut down to make a nice new door.

Horse Chestnut where life once sprang, from branch to branch
A fence post now on someone's ranch
Where sun shone through your great green head
Alas no more, now you are dead.

Great Ash you burn so bright
On the fire of the night
The hedgerow looks so grim and bare
Now your presence is no longer there.

Beech tree who offered shelter and shade
I wonder where you were laid
You stood so proud in a sunlit glade
Pianos and music you are made.

Maple in autumn coloured the best
Nature's hand has so finely dressed
Cut down to make a fine new chair
Do we think of you when we sit there?

Walnut, you are so kind
You share your gifts at Christmas time
When we have so much fun
Alas, you're felled - to make a gun!

Elm, you are dressed right to the floor
Alas, you are no more
Your wood is used for coffins and war
Killed forever by a beetle's bore.

John William Bowen

Harvest - 1930s

As fields of corn sway in the breeze
Now ripened by the sun
No time for men to rest at ease
For harvest has begun

Labourers start with scythes held steady
And cut a track quite wide
When this is done the field is ready
For the binder to move inside

Shire horses have the machine in tow
And set off round the track
Around and round the field they go
There is not time to slack

Sharpened blades slide to and fro
And cut the golden straw
Onward still the horses go
The machine cuts more and more

Although it's working at its best
And gets through quite a lot
It's time for man and horse to rest
As sun is burning hot

The horses have nosebags of bran
Then drink from stream nearby
While men swig tea from billy can
Or home-made beer they'll try

Refreshed, so now it's off they go
And start up once again
While men stack sheaves in row on row
To air the ripened grain

And though there's still lots must be done
There's quite a buzz you'd hear
As some folk wait with dog or gun
For rabbits may soon appear

With one stook left, no one can glean
To do so would be trouble
But once removed we'd pick field clean
And just leave all the stubble!

Derrick Wooding

I Love You

I love you dearly,
I love you so,
My love for you
Will always grow,

These words to you
I can't reveal,
As my heart beats faster,
But yet keeps still.

So let me hold you,
Firm and tight,
I want to be with you
Both day and night.

So be mine for now
And be mine forever,
So let us both
Just be together.

So here I end
This rhyme to be,
As I love you -
Do you love me?

Peter Barnes

Enchanted Forest

('The Enchanted Forest' by Derbyshire wildlife artist, Pollyanna Pickering, was painted in celebration of the 25th anniversary of the Born Free Foundation)

Bright eyed, he stands upon the wall
Hypnotic gaze, our hearts enthral
As we, beneath his spell, now fall
Enchanted

In light and shade, mysterious
Midst birch trees, staring, fearless
He seeks attention, peerless
Pack leader

Oh Wolf, were you born wild and free?
How Pollyanna's artistry
Has captured you for all to see
In gouache

Is it just imagination?
Vibrant life in your creation
Prompting such deliberation
Eyes follow

So Wolf, with us at Folly Well
Now you have come with us to dwell
A special tale of life you tell
And freedom.

Marilyn K Hambly

Lacuna

Under the old iron roof
they took shelter;
strangers brought together
by the elements.
The young girl, solemn
in her white blouse, the old
man shapeless of face and body,
his eyes far away from the cold.

He smiled at his new companion,
a big empty pillar box grin.
The girl shuddered
at a sight so alien.

Exhausted from his walk,
he lay quietly on the stone floor.
Outside, the grey mushroom clouds
threatened fountains of tears.

From a dreamless sleep
he awoke to find her gone,
and as he raised himself
from his makeshift bed
he knew she'd taken him
to be the sum of his guise;
and even in her silence
enough was said.

Anne Palmer

With Love In Your Heart

Reach out to your brother
Hold a hand out in friendship
Love one another

Give a little kindness
As you go from day to day
Send out your light
Give peace and give love
To help them on their way

A smile costs nothing
It's easy to share
What a great way of showing another you care

Spend a little time
Live your life with feeling
The world in all its sadness
Needs a lot of healing

Make a pledge!
Start today!
Others may follow
If you lead the way.

Rita Dilks

The Herald

I did not understand dream bird was death's dread herald,
The forest of my soul invaded by the bird's beauty;
Ethereal, liquid notes, the angelic host no purer,
Such bliss divine, exquisite, such music unimagined;
The shallow world had vanished, the brink of heaven reaching,
Long days of torment ended and rapture found at last.

Who were you, blessed bird, your soaring soul in ecstasy?
No nightingale or skylark ever sang so sweetly.

And yet, I would not question, drowned content in beauty,
Enveloped, saturated, such joyful anguish found.
My prayer, for peace perfected, for peace to last for ever,
In harbour, safe and calm, my weary searchings over.

Oh agony supreme when sleep at length was ended,
When melody had faded, the music not remembered.
This bliss a dream divine? My waking soul revolted.
Sing, sing again, blest bird, life arid, drear without you.

Vain plea, vain hope, all vain; why were my eyes so blinded?
This heralder of death, long feared but long expected -
A fleeting glimpse of heaven before heaven claimed her own.

Dorothy Jean Stirland

If I Had The Power

My pen would be mightier than the sword,
Politics may come and go,
Yet the harm to people is for generations to know,
Parents, our children are precious,
Each one as they grow,
If I had the power our troops would not suffer so.

To defend our own country is all we should ask of them,
Brave our lads and lasses are I know.
Yet the politicians never send their sons to die,
So bring them home,
Lord's sake, get them all out,
God please tell us what it's all about.

As a child, before they were born
I suffered in World War II,
We knew then it was to defend us,
Yet is it now our war?
More harm has it done,
Ask all in our country and send them home soon.

I slept each night, below ground, in air raid shelters,
My childhood friend, Madge Airie, by bombers one night
Was killed with her grandmother in a raid up in Hull.
My children and grands, I watch them when I can,
At only six years I was taken from our garden by an evil man,
'If I Had The Power', like Esther Rantzen, August 2009
Child cruelty forever *gone* with help from charity Childline.

Zena Foster

Towards A Better Time

Peace hides behind a wall built by fear,
In a far away place, where all thought the end was near,
Where faith is worth more than gold,
But try telling that to men with hearts so cold.
Peace is the key to many doors
But war is the key to Hell.
Hope is a story lost in time
That no one will dare to tell.
In a world with a thousand voices,
Lies a path with only two choices,
Happiness with you has come like a bird from the sky,
But my words are for you and will never lie.
When you laugh I look at you and I can see you crying,
When the sun begins to set,
I know, this time, I won't be dying.

Jonathan Gilbert

The Cherry Tree

We sat beneath the cherry tree
My own true love and I
He picked me sweet red cherries
With the taste of ambrosial wine
And all around was a breathless hush
The world seemed to stop its turning
As I gazed into eyes of burning blue
And my heart began its yearning
We talked and laughed as lovers do
He promised me his undying love
And a heart that would always be true
We left that place of youthful bliss
Two hearts as one entwining, secret place we found
We'll go back to that place
And the love forever enduring.

Doris May Hyde

This Thing

This thing is given freely,
It comes right from the heart,
Whether you live together
Or whether you live apart.
You only know you have it,
When you're feeling warm inside,
When you've shared a lot of pleasure,
With a friend you can confide.
It doesn't matter, young or old,
We all have lots to give,
So keep giving generously,
Much happier then you'll live.
When it's returned and comes your way
You get that heavenly feeling,
With a great big smile upon your face,
It's with your heart you're dealing.
My darling, you're the man for me,
Sent from Heaven above,
So I give to you most willingly,
This wonderful thing called love.

Kathleen Egan

The Line

A new age begins.
He paints, paint on paint.
Line, continually repainted.
White, straight even narrower.
Edges sharp, clearly defined,
Essential if the traveller
Is not to be derailed.

Ivan Langham

21st Birthday

A twenty-first birthday means many things
You've been to school, maybe uni too.
Apart from the day you were born
This is a great step for you.

Many horizons are open to you,
Maybe find that pot of gold!
Do what you think you would like
And let the future unfold.

So here's a drink for what's ahead,
Work hard, play hard too.
Make friends and care for others
But please, always be you!

Forward Press has come of age!
Twenty one we hear,
It's helped us many wannabe poets
So let's give them a cheer.

Writing a poem for some is hard,
For them it's a new beginning.
We trip ourselves up many times,
But soon we think we're winning!

So don't be despondent, that's a must,
We are a newborn breed!
So try, try, try again
And you will soon succeed.

Good luck to all.

C Greed

Angel In Despair

I saw the crumpled figure
Lying there,
Crying out in despair.
'I don't want to live, I want to die,
Someone to listen, someone to care.'
I reached out and took the frail little body in my arms,
'Hush,' I said, 'I am here, I love you dearly, I care.'
As I cuddled her close, her fragile bones almost breaking,
So was my heart.
I touched the once beautiful, angelic face,
Now wracked with alcohol, drugs and pain.
The once beautiful golden curls,
Now tangled and matted with neglect.
I stroked to soothe her troubled head,
'What a waste of young life,' I said,
'When all you wish is to be dead.
Life is precious, whatever it brings,
There is always another door to open,
So please little girl of mine,
Wake up and live.
Take my hand and come with me,
Back into the world of the living,
Life has so many wonderful things to see.'

Joanne Hattershun

Ringing In The New

Church bells ring out the old, ring in the new.
Last year has just finished,
The last stroke of twelve on the clock,
Where the big and small hands meet,
Pointing up to the heavens
And as they do, fireworks fill the sky,
Lighting up the rooftops,
Exploding into rainbows,
Announcing the first day of the New Year in celebration.
What will it hold?
As mother's give birth,
Babies' lungs inhale their first breath.
Proud fathers see their child for the very first time.
Couples get married
And exchange vows, exchange rings,
Church bells ring out in celebration.
Some people will be saddened by the loss of a loved one,
But there will always be kindly folk, with caring hearts
Who give their love and support to those who need it.
Life is a celebration, like the seasons of the year,
Spring, summer, autumn and winter,
Every day precious, live it to the full.

Linda Knight

Only One Belper

Strong in the arm,
weak in the head,
of Derbyshire folk
that once was said.
But now,
Belper, unique.
At the heart of Derbyshire,
the county so swinging,
the county so sweet.
Belper.
Once called Beaurepaire,
a private garden still carries that name,
Belper in Derbyshire
the only one in the land,
make that the world.
Nailers land
Cotton centre
Untamed beauty
That is Belper.

David Robinson

Simon de Montfort, Earl Of Leicester

Sleep you easy noble lord
Since your last breath in Evesham Vale?
Dream you of your Eleanor
The triumph of your stealthy match?
Kinship foisted on your king
And bask you in the wary praise
Of uncertain baronage
Wondering whose ends you served
Who might among them stand or fall?

Though time's selective memory
Allows your name to be revered;
A seat of learning named for you
A well respected concert hall;
There is a judge who heard the cries
Of those you causelessly oppressed
The helpless ones you dispossessed
And in that day we all must face
He'll know your Haman heart.

(Haman - the villain in the Old Testament book of Esther.)

Pamela Sanders

Travelling

What's it like to travel
On a helicopter in flight?
Or maybe on a ship
By day or by night?

Be in a vehicle on roads
Or travelling by train?
You've the chance of a ferry,
Or flying on a plane.

Listen to the tram,
Running on its track,
Climb up on a saddle
To go riding, horseback.

There are many ways to travel,
Whichever the way you like,
Go in a hot air balloon
Or even on a bike.

You've got water, rails,
Roads and air,
Please enjoy your journey
Regardless of the fare.

Rita Wilde

Blossoms

Oh England is a garden
So the poet's lyrics tell.
Rock and cranny, hill and fen
Wood and moor, river and dell
Hide the flowers that grow so free
Under the banks beneath the trees
Lifting their heads to the honeybee.
Nodding and swaying in the breeze,
Daisy, primrose and buttercup gay
Hedgerose, elder and sweet may.

Lilac and cherry and pink almond flower
Border the roses in a formal array.
Cool and inviting is my lady's bower
Delighting the eye with a charming display
Of fuschias, freesias and hollyhocks tall
Surrounded by pansies, carnations and stocks;
Purple clematis climb over the wall.
Down by the pool, among the rocks
London pride, lavender and lilies white
Bring to heart God's gentle might.

So the flowers, with their rainbow hues
Charm and enhance this fair land of ours.
A magic carpet of colour for all to view
A fragment of peace in the tumult of hours.
Guard this gift as among them you toil
They brave the storms all beauty to spoil.
Then the sun shine in his splendour again
Restoring the blossoms to perfection once more.

Lois Burton

Retirement

From fifteen to sixty I was employed.
Doing lots of jobs, some of which I enjoyed,
Typing in an office wasn't for me,
Factory fodder I then came to be.

We just followed like sheep, never questioned our lot,
Thankful for our jobs and the pay we got,
Had enough for our needs and paid our way,
Didn't question any further than the day to day.

Eventually, we saw the light,
We decided to stand and fight,
Equal rights for all and equal pay,
At last became the law of the day.

Now I have retired and am my own boss each day,
My time is my own, to do with as I may.

Brenda Reville

Journey Into Night

A sense of jewels, displayed on black velvet.
Out of reach patterns entering the beginning
On this starlit night, a planet floats.
Now, a journey into this place of utter silence reveals
A city of tall elegance.
There are structures, clouded, the colour of sand,
Existing now in space, drifting slowly, you
Appear in a mask of silence.
Alleyways curve seductively, disappearing as I pass.
I drift in this phantasmagoria I am unable to control.
World of mind passes into the shadowy abyss of this journey, where
Shapes of precise calculation float past gaunt alleyways, where
Sentinels of silence are mounting a huge canvas
Of naked humanity.
Veiled men on horseback fade in an instant, into
The castle of my dreams.

Richard Cluroe

Entertaining Spiders

Why do great big spiders
Run under my TV?
Is it to see the newsreader
Or to get away from me?

Do they love to watch 'Gardener's World'
When the day is gone,
So they can gaze in admiration
At the lovely Monty Don?

Perhaps they're Formula 1 fans,
'Top Gear's' the name of their game,
Or perhaps they fancy 'Come Dancing'
In Blackpool's hall of fame.

They usually come around seven
And under the telly they meet,
They're all lined up for 'EastEnders'
And never miss 'Corrie Street'.

They cannot stand the 'X Factor'
With all the din they make,
They'd rather wait for 'Match of the Day'
That keeps them wide awake.

When the match is over
They turn and make for home,
Just one at a time, out they come
Never more to roam.

For waiting with lots of patience
Is my terrier, named Jack
And if he missed them going in
He'll sure catch them coming back.

He picks them up and chews them,
Spits them out, rolls on them with his head,
When he's done this a few times
He makes sure that they're *dead!*

Tomorrow, just around seven
In they come, march over the floor,
Under the TV they will go,
There must be three or four.

But where do they all come from
And how do they know where to go?
Where to get free entertainment,
But little do they know,

There's someone waiting for them
After they've seen the show.
So enjoy yourselves my beauties
For there's nowhere else to go.

Hazel Palmer

Paths To Light

Where will my love find me in this darkness?
The forest is dark all around me,
Forest paths are all awry
How can my love find me in forest gloom?
Darkness has descended, no lights to see by,
Forest paths are all awry.
Never has my love
Found me in this gloom,
No moonglow to see,
Shadows none to show,
Forest paths are all awry.
Call my light, my love
To show you through the gloom,
See the sun break the sky,
No shadows to block your way,
Forest paths are clear.
Find me my love,
I look for you every day,
There is light everywhere.
See, I am there standing
Forest paths, I am there.

Ian Cresswell

Last Time Leaving

Christmas brought changes as she sat amongst her belongings,
Head spinning from the strange goings on inside it.
Perfectly lucid,
Trying to hold on to her dignity and freedom, independent to the last.
She would not consider hospital,
Waste of time to ask.

Finally, begrudgingly, in a faltering voice
she spoke with slurred words,
The ones she hoped she'd never utter.
Her worst nightmare was coming true,
Whilst consoling herself by telling others,
I'm only doing this for you.

Just a week they said,
She thought, *I'd manage that.*
But, as the days went by, she knew in her heart
She was caught in a trap.
With a body that was giving up,
It couldn't do the things she visualised in her head.
Walking with legs that have forgotten how to go,
Dragging a few steps, oh so slow,
Unable to get into bed or out
Without help, that seemed so long in coming,
In answer to her ringing bell or final, impatient shout.

She listened while they told her,
'You couldn't manage in your home,
Best you stay here to be cared for; you're a danger on your own.'
She didn't care about the risk, one thing she knew for sure,
All she wanted was to go back home, not live here anymore.

When fear and grief overwhelmed her,
she behaved in a myriad of ways,
Snapping, snarling at those who cared,
while knowing that way never pays.
In the silence of her alien room, strange in the darkness of the night,
She prayed to her God and pleaded for release from her plight.
The days went by and slowly she gave up her final battle,
Joined the others dosed with pills, so many she felt she would rattle.

She thought she could put on a brave face;
pretend she'd accepted her state,
Yet, every evening, alone, she cried, desperate tears from her heart.
Lord, tell me, what did I do to deserve this as my final part, my fate?

Freda Straw

I'll Never Understand

I'll never understand
Why you had to go away
It's so very hard without you
Every second of every day
The love I have for you
Will never die or even fade
Lots of special memories
Together! We have made
If I could have one wish come true
It would be reaching out and holding you
The special days we cannot share
A daily thought with a silent prayer
But in my heart is where you'll stay
Until we meet again some day
Those gates of Heaven are open wide
To let in this precious friend of mine
Reach out and touch those soft, gentle hands
But losing you is what
I cannot understand!

I laugh, I smile and I play the part
But our true friendship is kept here
Deep within my heart.

Annamarie Yates

At The Cross

It is at *the cross*, where I must not forget
It is at *the cross,* where if troubled I can come

At *the cross* I can lay my burdens down
I can bring my inner fears
I can ask, 'Lord, help me.'
I can ask 'Help me to be.'
I can ask 'I have for a moment, fallen short.'
I can ask 'Please forgive me Lord.'
I can ask, 'Help me to walk as You wish.'
I can ask, 'Help me to be humble in Your sight.'

I can be honest for God is listening
I can bring my weakness for God knows the time of fall
I can bring others in prayer.

At *the cross,* a special place, where when troubled or in need
Of a touch of love, we can come and our troubles are shared.

Barbara Fletcher

The Battle Of The Sexes - Won?

'The hand that rocks the cradle is the hand that rules the world.'
'Each successful man has a wife who stands behind.'
the poets declaimed our status and made recognition plain -
the female sex is capable and kind.

We were there at the beginning, Creation's very start
Constructed only seconds after man
And in our Maker's blueprint, faultlessly and clear
Equality of the sexes was the plan.

The bid for some acknowledgement of value and of worth
Has been a battle, wearisome and long
Patience was the handle to achieve our lawful end
Not this weapon which has placed us in the wrong.

We have now - perverse reversal - observed the status change
Successful men now cower behind the wife
The hand that rocks the cradle is most evilly intent
On snuffing out the little, helpless life.

Gillian Beardow

Determination

What is the real purpose of education?
It can prepare us for a profession or vocation.
But on its own, it will never be enough,
It must be coupled with drive and determination.

For education can fill out mind with information
Sufficient for us to pass the school examination,
But if we want to obtain a degree in the university of life
We have to overcome the problems associated with strife.

For life is not a game of Blind Man's Buff,
Knowledge on its own will never be enough,
We should not sit back and let life evolve,
We must show determination and resolve.

For education is nothing more than a tool,
Which we can all get by going to school,
But it is the folk who show guts and determination
Who, in the long run, will protect the future of our nation.

Ronald Martin

Live For The Moment

We can't re-live our yesterdays,
those of golden beaches
and nights which left us speechless,
stumbling over the right words to say,
yet all we can do is try to stay,
stay positive,
realise our options
and live,
be it for the second, hour or moment,
as these times forge memories
never to be broken.

Gavin Cooke

The Colour Of Confession

Black.
Not coal-black
Or the black of ink,
But the total absence of light.
I've mastered the dark long since.

Dust.
Hangs in the air
Slips into my veins.
A carnelian arc of death,
The final blow is struck.

Blame.
Not mine alone
Or yours to hold,
But hers in her peacock vanity,
Knowing neither humility or shame.

Ruby.
Her silhouette
Floats in ethereal orbit,
But meets the Earth in prose
And her debris creates a halo of red.

Breath.
It is stifled,
Stifled by that which I have done,
But no burden to bind
Others would have done the same.

Hate.
An unpleasant colour
To wear upon one's sleeve.
A crimson bruise
Fanning across a blackening pit.

Dust.
Damned spot upon me;
That she should bring me to this.
But my soul is choking
In my secret delight.

Smile.
Coughing,
My hand too slow to reach my mouth.
But here expands that firebrick circle
Where I fall and smile in my triumph.

Susie Crozier

A Moonlit Night

On high, Diana
The turner of tides
And starter of cycles
Looks down, luminous.
Moths dance in her light,
Seeking union from
The shadows.
Brock's humbug face
Appears among the hyacinth,
Snuffling and snorting,
His dusted nose samples the air.
The owl hisses distaste
His hunt ruined, floats
On silent wings to his roost.
A bark from the sly one
Signals his nightly scrounge,
Disappearing through the trees.
Bats fly on parchment wings,
Madly dodging obstacles.
On bright pasture rabbits nibble
Boldly, with eyes aglint
And ears twitching.
While mice scurry noisily
Among the leaves
Washed with moonlight.

Mark Marsden

The Nothing Day

The day the sun refused to shine,
when folk can't say, 'The weather's fine.'
No fog, so we can see our way.
No breeze to make the washing sway.
No rain to spoil a summer's trip
or frost around for Jack to nip.
No snow to give the young a thrill.
It's just a day that's still as still.
No hurling hail to damage crops.
Or slashing sleet when humour drops.
No thunder rumbling round the skies.
No lightning shocks our frightened eyes.
I feel no sweat of burning ray
for this is just a nothing day.

Margaret Edge

21st Birthday

A poem for this birthday
Not as hard as you may think!
This put on my shoulders; responsibility
Would be depression; to sink?

To do a poem for this
Comes quite easily to me
Read my book of poems
Hopefully then you'll see!

Forward Press has opened up
A brand new world for everyone!
Go, take up your pen
Or inspiration will be long gone!

Simone Summerscales

Clean/Serene

It's raining, feels like venom
Cold acupuncture needles
Penetrate through my clothes
Thirsty Nature absorbs it all in
Sodden soil and drenched flowers

Growing, always growing

The sky, bruised with whiteness shown
These are the worst of days
When dark descends in rapid falls
It feels like the last days
On this vast plain drenched in pity

Yet clean and serene
Washing the dirt away

The colour of the trees in full bloom
Virgin forest where birds are free
I long for the warmth of the new sun
Lazy, hot days in minimal clothes
Women with warm sun-baked flesh.

Steven Michael Pape

Obituary

(Brianostamus Plecostamus)

Brian's gone, no more I see his gob
Pressed against glass like some unseemly yob,
Feeding on what algae he could glean
As the walls of his prison he sucked clean.

Yes, Brian's gone; perhaps something he ate.
For him no Christian word nor closing hymn,
But for his sins, quick flip of rusty plate
And into County Council wheelie bin!

They named him after me - I know not why,
Perhaps the gormless gape, the baleful eye?
I'm glad he's gone, for no more shall I see
That fish, they said reminded them of me!

Brian Large

Her Name Was Anna Palk

How to describe a dream girl, who in life you never met?
An actress of stage, film and television, whose photo you had to get.
The first time that I saw her was in 'The Main Chance', on TV
And Anna had a charisma that certainly appealed to me.
So, I sent away for a photo, I told her that I wished for
And over the many years after, Anna sent me quite a few more.
Anna said that she hated letter writing, but mine just made her laugh,
In time I became her favourite fan, she wrote this on a photograph.
She did write to me many times after, but suddenly contact did end,
But it seemed Anna had an illness and expired, so I lost a very dear friend.
Anna left this world much too early, her age being just forty-seven,
But there's a beautiful angel above now,
there in God's Holy Heaven.
She will always remain in my heart and my thoughts,
of that I am just sure,
For Anna was such a wonderful person
and her memory will always endure.
Photographs on view, recalling a friendship
That you hope had been made,
Holding a remembrance, with times past, that to me, they will not fade.
And so, this simple message, from her favourite fan,
so enraptured by her face,
But words cannot really capture her charm, her persona, her grace.
It's now been over forty years since sending for the first photograph,
Maybe Anna is looking down and saying,
'John, you still make me laugh!'

John Franks

If

(A husband's last words to his dying wife)

If I could do anything
To take away your pain
Darling, I would do my best
To make you well again

If the world was like a garden
And dreams could grow like weeds
I'd pick one every hour
And banish all your needs

If I could take one moment
And freeze it for all time
I'd freeze the time you said, 'I do'
When you, at last, became mine

But, alas, I cannot do these things
No matter how I try
Though I'll never give up hoping
Until the day you die

That day I will not say, 'Goodbye'
I'll merely say 'Adieu'
Until the day we meet again
I'll never stop loving you
So when you get to Heaven
Free from all your pain
Save me a seat beside you
Then we can love again.

W Currie

Computer Dating

We share magic moments through cyber space
Strange feelings inside, my heart starts to race
I'm falling for you without seeing your face
Mystery man on the Internet

I get flutterbyes when you use my name
I often wonder if you feel the same
We talk through the night, so much more than a game
Mystery man on the Internet

Introduced by strangers on a website
A strange way to meet but it somehow feels right
I tell you I love you, I think that I might
Mystery man on the Internet

Our friendship is something that's special to me
What the future holds I just wait to see
Will we meet one day is for fate to decree
Mystery man on the Internet.

Rachel Sidebottom

Soldier, Soldier

We are proud of our soldiers who go out to war,
They fight for their country with honour and more,
We watched them march past, so smart, with such class,
We gave them our support and cheered as they passed.
The career they have chosen is tough and with fight,
With all kinds of dangers and unknown future in sight,
But the homecoming is exciting, the atmosphere great,
Everyone's happy and waiting at the gate!
Forward Press, let's pop the corks and celebrate,
The People's Publisher has come of age,
One million or more poems have been published so far,
Congrats Forward Press, we look forward to more.

Dulcie E Walker Miranda

The Forest

Sunlight merrily dancing amongst the shadowy trees,
But my heart did not feel it.

Birds singing in different voices, creating their operatic music,
But my ears did not hear it.

Rich, royal, autumn colours with beauty beyond belief,
But my eyes did not see them.

Sweet smells of bark and leaves lingering in the air,
But whose fragrance passed me by.

Textures, various and wonderful, of fallen twigs,
But they did not touch my senses.

Running water cascading down through a gap in the trees,
But its beauty I could not speak.

The forest's mighty presence not appreciated,
No sense to feel its healing quality.

But then I opened my mind and let in its purity
And I saw, heard, felt, touched and spoke its power.

My heart could live again
And I believed in life once more.

Deb Thurland

I Miss You

No one knows
Just how much I miss you
No one knows
Just how much it hurts
For the pain is deep inside
And the tears I cry won't go away
I know, because I've tried
That's why no one knows
Just how much it hurts
To lose you -
My beloved twin sister.

Ella Wright

The Year's Medley

Spring kicked up her heels
And bounced merrily along,
Shooting up in leaps and bounds.
In lanes and fields and gardens
Splashing green here, there and everywhere,
In a seemingly haphazard fashion.

Rolling in great waves over hillsides,
Hedges and down into valleys.
Then back up again into the trees.
Just for added devilment
Sprinkled dazzling patches of yellow
That sang out the sun's reflected rays.

It made lambs and all young things skittish,
To older ones added a spring to their step.
Everything was burgeoning forth
In the great race to be first
To announce the arrival of Spring.

Spring steadied into a rosy pink
Then rolled slowly over into Summer.

Summer offered a cold shoulder
To show she was not at all impressed
By this young upstart,
Though, at times, she flickered
A wan, half-accepting smile,
Then sank back beneath her grey mantle again, to sulk.
But encouraged by Time's impatience
Burst forth in golden rays, hot and fiery,
To follow in Spring's traces.
Lambs slowed down, all steps slowed,
The yellow faded to be replaced by a Persian carpet,
Scented with exotic perfumes that sent busy bees
Into a fumbling, tumbling ecstasy.

Sea and sky turned blue and sparkled,
Sand became golden,
Everything revelled in Summer's empowering warmth,
Everything was easy.
Birds sang, children played, people of all ages came
Worshipped the sun and relaxed.

Summer tired, her energy spent, she sat back
And mellowed into Autumn.

Autumn rejoiced in Summer's retirement
And decked the Earth with gold and scarlet.
Then gave up the bounteous harvest
Endowed by Summer's wealth.
Trees and hedgerows hung heavily with the ripened fruits.
Great tidal waves of gold rippled over fields.
This great provender was gathered up
To nourish Man and beast.

Autumn then ambled like a grey, misty, old man
Into Winter.

Winter received it and added dozens of its own.
Old, stark and gnarled, standing gaunt, denuded of youth.
The earth entrenched itself against Winter's onslaught,
It subdued everything with its cold, probing fingers.
Freezing all with its icy touch.

The anger of its lost youth and its mouldering old age
Buried deep in its stone-cold heart.
Now blasted round every corner,
Into every nook, as it vented its rage.
Streams and rivers stopped flowing,
Birds stopped singing,
Flowers quivered beneath the earth.
Nothing stirred, only the violent winds,
Trees stood like bowing sentinels against the wild fury.

Then, in deep repentance, Winter stopped, stood back,
Stared a long, dark, cold stare on the havoc it had rent.
Realised the uselessness of its cause,
Robed itself in virgin white and glitteringly bejewelled
Went forth and sacrificed itself to Spring.

Spring accepted Winter with her gentle warmth,
Melted its cold heart,
Then, sighing, gently, kicked up her heels and bounced merrily along.

Anne Bailey

Passing Shadows

Bathed in moonlight now sleeps the Earth,
Soft shadows at twilight surround her girth.
Wind whispers and the trees sway,
Nocturnal creatures wend their way.

Gentle stillness over all,
Far away the owl gives call.
The distant rumbling of a train
Passes like a shower of rain.
Whilst stars, like sequins, twinkle and shine,
Pouring down their light with a glow sublime.

Dawn rises with a sense of chill,
Pervading the Earth and the air is still.
Sun rises like an overture,
Brightening the sky a little more.

The promise of a sunny day
Chases the night shadows all away
And the sleepless night owls
Wing back to their nest,
Till once again the sun goes to her rest.

Pat Langton

The Things I Have Found

There's a smile in the air
And a chuckle in the sea,
The sun keeps on laughing
As fat clouds drift merrily.

Before I never noticed
What went on all around;
Now you're here, it's amazing
The things that I have found.

A scarecrow's always grinning
Though he's standing in the rain,
And a bird keeps on singing
As he swoops to eat the grain.

Before I never noticed
What went on all around;
Now you're here, it's amazing
The things that I have found.

The river's shining silver
With reflections from the moon,
The stars are turning cartwheels
Bright as the flowers that bloom.

Before I never noticed
What went on all around;
Now you're here, it's amazing
The things that I have found.

Hazel Deathridge

Friendship In The New Dawn

(Based on John's Gospel, chapter 21)

'Simon are you my friend?' You know O Lord,
You know the many miles I walked with You,
Through toil and danger, three whole glorious years
Of sick folk healed and words of joy proclaimed.
I followed You the hard and lonely way
Up to the city where Your suffering lay.
I stayed beside You on that dark, dread night,
When you went forth alone, to face in prayer
The bitter trial that lay ahead for You.
But still I stayed beside You, loyal and true
Right to the judgement hall - where I failed You.'

'Peter, I know. You've one more thing to learn,
No more remorse or agony of soul,
For you have just the quality I need
In my true shepherd of my faithful flock.
True love is friendship, lasting, loyal, strong,
The friendship that God has for me and you.'

Never, in fact, was there a greater friend
Than our dear Lord, who saw the needs of all
And noticed others' pain as He passed by,
Who wept beside His friends and showed to men
The greatest gift of all that God can give -
A faithful friend who died that we might live.

For friendship is a lovely, gracious thing,
Devoted, loyal, abiding, free and true,
The sacred privilege of burdens shared
And sorrows halved, of echoed thoughts and words,
Responsive minds and troubles understood,
That finds at last its greatest joy has lain -
In caring.

Sheila Harris

Credit Crunch Kid

I am a Credit Crunch kid
I live in a Credit Crunch Town
The worn-out clothes that I wear
Are from Oxfam or hand-me-down

There are many derelict shops here
Down our dirty, pot-holed street
I sail my paper boats
And splash about with my feet

There are supermarkets and car parks here
But the playing fields have all gone
And the shops are now all empty
These days few shiny cars come

My father says negative equity
Is partly to blame for it all
As against a boarded-up window
I kick an old, tattered ball

The money's all dried up now
There's no sign of work about yet
Will this nightmare ever end?
Still I must try not to fret

Maybe tomorrow will be better
Perhaps I won't be so alone
I'll make a new life for myself
Grow up and have kids of my own

Perhaps they will all laugh then
At the sad things that I did
As I tell them of the times
When I was a Credit Crunch kid.

Richard F Magan

Your Village Church

I am your village church,
For centuries I've stood
And watched the people come and go
Both the wicked and the good.

My chancel is 1200
My stained glass is very fine,
One archway's date is Norman
But the font's is lost in time.

My bells ring every Sunday
Their message loud and clear,
Calling you to worship and
The Almighty's word to hear.

My organ's been restored
And the lovely notes are pure,
A sound of joyful welcome
As you approach my ancient door.

When you kneel in silent prayer
In a medieval pew,
Think of all the other souls
Who've knelt there before you.

Constant years of praises sung,
Thanksgiving from age to age
Have left a special aura
As history turned each page.

I've witnessed many marriages
But for me the greatest joy
Has been the infant christening
Of every girl and boy.

At all the village weddings
Tears of happiness are shed
And again they fall in sorrow
At the burial of the dead.

There have been so many wars
And I have watched with pain,
To see the young men leaving
Who've not come home again.

In World War II no bells rang out,
Of invasion they would warn,
But loud and long the peals did come,
When peace at last was born.

My clock, which ticks life's time away,
From high up on the tower,
Waits for no one, like the tide
And strikes with mellow note each hour.

By my path the tombstones stand,
Testament to men's lives
And often lower down the stone
A brief addition for their wives.

Beside my gate a yew tree grows,
With its branches spreading wide
And nearby flower the snowdrops
Having winter's cold defied.

Later on the daffodils
Come out at Easter time,
Followed by the cherry trees
With their blossom so sublime.

Now, if suddenly, I vanished,
Leaving just an empty space,
I wonder, would you notice,
Would you miss this sacred place?

I expect you'd miss the clock,
As you often check the time
And possibly the bells as well
For I know you like the chime.

You feed your body, train your mind
And make efforts to keep fit,
But you forget about your soul,
The everlasting bit.

Our Lord is the Good Shepherd
And He loves His straying sheep,
But they need to be inside His fold,
In His eternal keep.

Jane Walker-Okeover

White Noise

(To D.L.)

This is your rollercoaster
your whole body experience
not mine
but the downdraught
and the mood-waves
catch me
toss me
envelope me;
the turbulence constant
the all-encompassing force fierce;
and always the undercurrents
the unknown
dip-whirls suck whorls;
unprepared the mind grey-blanks
deep gorge banks
buffeting its way
in up round
and round
trapped in an endless
cacophony of white noise . . .

Bette Walklate

The Struggle

Disquietude clings fast to thy brain,
With roots deep-clenched and fruits sour,
These doubts thy every thought do stain
And those few certainties that remain,
They weaken by the hour.

These black and bitter thoughts, they feed
Despair and render thy pain stark,
Till apathy becomes thy creed
And the world, once loved, turns dark.

All thy friends have thou rejected
And of thy passions thou art shorn;
In thine eyes is sorrow reflected
And night revokes the dawn.

But none can see what has begun,
Deep within thy throbbing heart,
Where joy is dead and hope is wan
And all thy dreams shall soon depart.

Now a look of woe is impressed,
Skull-deep upon thy weary brow
And sadness on thine heart is pressed
So fiercely that it longs to rest,
Yet struggles on somehow.

Carl Carter

British Summer

There is nothing like a British Summer
Nice to see all the flowers
Who are much happier than us
To receive all the showers

Better half says, 'Please, no digging,'
Though it's what the garden needs
Because she says, 'Being just a man
You can't tell flowers from weeds!'

The rain means hedge needs cutting more
And that is quite a labour
I'm unable to reach the top
Thank God I've a lovely neighbour.

Think what the alternative to rain would be
With a summer drought
Walking up and down with watering cans
I'd rather have rain than nowt!

Bernie Adams

Red Roses

So occupied in life's monotony,
I spared no thought nor dared to ruminate
On unforeseen disasters that await,
To pounce and pierce my heart impassively,
Benumb and wrest my happiness from me;
How could fate be unkind and desecrate
Our hallowed world and thus obliterate
Our union by her brutality?

But memories live in each crimson rose,
Fed on unceasing love, a million tears;
Abundant, unsurpassed, their beauty grows,
Rich fragrance soothes and sorrow disappears;
Red petals fall, snatched by a breeze that blows
Them heavenward to undiscovered spheres.

Hilary J Cairns

Fiftieth Wedding Anniversary

Okay, you fell out of love years ago
When I look into your dear old face
I have to think that this was so.

You think that I'll be feeling low
But I will handle this with grace
Okay, you fell out of love years ago

When we were young our love would grow
Divorce was never going to be the case
I have to think that this was so

We thought the daily ebb and flow
Would make us strong to stay the pace
Okay, you fell out of love years ago

I ask myself, did you never know
I was the one who held the ace?
I have to think that this was so

So now our love has lost its glow
We have moved to another base
Okay, you fell out of love years ago
I have to think that this was so.

Joy Wright

Autumn

A rosary of wild geese
Cast in narrowing skeins
Across a morning sky
Patched with dark cloud-wrack
Promises, in aerial pilgrimage
The hope of warmer, southern skies
For those of us who have to face
An iron winter.

Derek Oakley

Ist July 1916 - To The Fallen

They said it would be a walkover,
That everything would be OK
The bombardment so terrible
That Jerry would not want to stay.

It had gone on for days
The rumbling thunder of the many big guns
No one would survive to hear the lark
As we arose that morning to our advance
It was going to be but a walk in the park.

As it got dark I couldn't sleep
My nerves a'tremble for the coming day
With thoughts of loved ones, of many goodbyes
That troubled me deep
I did drift off somewhere
For how long, I couldn't say.

I dreamt of reading newspapers on top of each other
Of many headlines of omen, *60,000 dead* one said,
Over 70,000 fall on the first day, another
It was then I knew that I'd soon be dead.

The nerves had gone, a numb peace instead
A feeling of joy, somehow stronger,
That I'd done this before, not to worry
After death I need fear no danger.

The sun, dirty orange, broke cover
Over misty dugouts far away
A lark spiralled eagerly upward to the sky,
I realised this was it, this was the day
The last I'd see, for I would die.

The bugles blared and whistles blew
As I climbed, scrambling over the top
My boots, muddy, wet with fresh dew
On that July morning still fresh.

We strode forward in the long grass
Past our fallen, hanging on barbed-wire mesh
I heard the thud and crack of hot lead pass
The woodpecker's notes of death, so distant,
Thudding, biting up the ground afresh
I ducked down in an instant.

I arose as a friend fell, near a shattered tree
Racing up I pulled him behind it
To get him out of harm into safety,
He was alive, wounded but winded they'd say
So I grasped his hand and got off the floor
As the medics came to take him away,
I arose and turned to walk on
A thud! A sudden flash!
I was no more.

Andrew Watts

At Heaven's Gate

At Heaven's gate
I stand and wait
For you my love
To come to me

At Heaven's gate
I think of my life
And give my thanks
That I found you

At Heaven's gate I see your face
Your tears of sorrow
Your broken heart

At Heaven's gate
By day or night
I long to be
Right by your side.

Tracey Jane Taylor

Recollections

It is Sunday morning.
From my Godmother's house, with her two children
We go to watch Mrs Shemwell, plaiting
The long hair of Betty and Ellen.
After the doleful drone of the beckoning bell
The gentle ebb and flow of singing becomes a billow.
The organ's crescendos, with the might of waves, surge and swell.
The service ends with Father Joyce's Alleluia solo.
We pass Holymoor House on our way to the dam,
There black tadpoles wriggle near the water's edge.
Coot, moorhen and mallard dabble where bathers swam
Close to pink lady smock, rush and sedge.
We cross the wooden bridge to the meadow
Where lush, green grass provides clover-scented hay.
The farmer like his forbears long ago
Pats his horses as, with a whinny and a neigh,
They pull the last load to the stack.
The lads drain the dregs of dandelion and burdock.
The farmer mops his brow and rubs his aching back.
At home there's laughter, it's Richard Murdoch
In 'Much Binding In The Marsh', on the radio.
Maman drops chopped mint leaves into vinegar and brown sugar
Decorates a cake with angelica and pistachio.
In the afternoon we walk up Windy Fields to Chander.
On gateposts white chalk arrows still remain.
Last week the Brownies went tracking,
Some went with Brown Owl down Pocknedge Lane.
Later Tawny Owl's group began following,
At Woodhead Farm the track led by the duck pond,
It was fun finding a letter and a drawing in a wall.
It showed Hallcliff brook and the path beyond.
At dusk the girls returned to the village hall.
Sixty years on, some see the sun set far, far away,
Its golden rays unite them in friendship to this day.

Vivienne Brocklehurst

The Shopping Trolley

Well here we are, it is Friday once more,
Another battle on the supermarket floor,
All the tins and packets lined up, looking jolly,
But lurking at the entrance, the dreaded shopping trolley.

It gets pushed into your back and run over your toes,
Why do people do it? Nobody knows.
Ouch! Look out that one caught my shins,
'Oh sorry dear,' comes the reply with that silly grin.

The shelves seem enormous and you stretch up high,
It feels like you're shopping in the sky.
Then you drop it and it lands on the floor,
Now who's moved the trolley? If they do that once more!

The trolley, now full of what you require,
You're feeling quite harassed and now getting tired,
But the worst isn't over, just look at the queue, your feet and head throbbing,
You want to go home, you feel like sobbing.

So home you go feeling all battered and blue,
Kids and hubby waiting, asking, 'What happened to you?
What's that bruise and how've you laddered your tights?
What on Earth have you been doing Mum! Have you been in a fight?'

The only fight I had today was down the road, not a mile away,
I know when I left I was feeling quite jolly
But I've just been to the supermarket with

The dreaded shopping trolley.

Dee Degnan

Meditation

Time holds out its hands
offering gifts, as fruit on trees,
gifts remembered as a child
when the world shone deeper
with the vibration of wonder,
filling fresh spring air
with silks of dawn
swirling over dewed grass
when you ran, feet bare,
listening to each birdsong
spiralling its melody
above a green, green garden,
to splash in sun,
perfume rising like incense,
colours moving like dreams.

Rain falls, glittering its necklace
into my open hands
before copper sunset retreats
dancing into blue-black night
threaded with stars
to turn again,
calling me from safety of sleep
to receive another gift.

Vivien Steels

First Years

I know now that these memories are
never going to be erased.
The darkness of the evening as it drew in
against us, on the top floor, writing about
databases and normalisation, young first years.
We called it the romantic glow of the seminar room
and joked about dirty things, double entendres,
a connection through those October nights.
Sometimes you would drive me home, the ten
miles to my house, even though it was just
ten minutes to yours from the university. We would
joke about getting lost on a dark road somewhere,
and other nights, I would take the bus home when it
wasn't too dark and I would walk from the bus stop
to my house. I'd be okay, I would be
listening to music and thinking of you,
and now I know when I listen to those songs, it's true
I know now that these memories are
imprinted in my brain, like those dark evenings,
which are drawing in again
and make me think of all these things.

Samantha Rose

The Spirit In The Rain

I have been inside
November rain
when the mist rises
from the earth;
heard the crack
inside the branch,

Smelt the sodden leaves
denuded trees
filled with a sudden burst
of gunfire
rip through the silence
I had found.

A breathless sigh
I came to meet
as feathers snowed
towards my feet,
rifle pointed at my head
wondered if the bird was dead.

I am November rain
the mist you cannot see
rising from the earth
to haunt the hunters -
haunting me.

Suzette Virginia Floyed

My 21st Birthday

To be away from home on your birthday -
Not good - I hear you say.
I had tuberculosis,
And in a sanatorium I had to stay.

From 20 and half a year to Switzerland I was sent,
A whole year there I spent.
Everyone joined with me on my special day,
Nurses, doctors, patients all came to say
Happy birthday to me.

Record requests on the hospital radio were played,
A lovely tea was laid.
Even a birthday cake from home was sent,
It arrived a bit broken and bent.
But we ate it all, and had a ball.

That day I'll remember all my life,
Now I'm a mother and a wife,
Thanks I give to the staff of long ago,
Grateful to be here today at 78, so

Happy birthday 21, to you, Forward Press,
Many more years will poetry live I guess.
While you are here to encourage and praise,
A glass to you I raise.

Iris Burgess

The Fool

I overheard some fool today
Escaping from the million feet
That daily tread each littered street,
Muttering as he made his way
Of true and everlasting love.

I laughed at such stupidity to say
A love like his could never die,
Would overcome the toll of years
Because together they defy
Sickness, poverty and the countless tears
To which our greatest poets testify.

Love has its first and final days
Like months or years or holidays –
In loving others we but love ourselves,
Take our loves and pleasures
As we choose books, from shelves,
Or press remote controls on our TV
For channels we prefer to see.
According to our current whim
We look with greater interest
On the hidden charms of her or him,
Then, growing weary, would divest
Ourselves in favour of some newer thing.

We take on loves as trees their leaves,
Let them grow dull and then release
Them seasonally as we please;
And any who would die for love
Show less constancy in their talk
Than have the shapes of clouds above
This leafy park wherein I walk
And where I choose to mutter on,
Regardless of the setting sun
And curious strollers passing by
A madman's late soliloquy.

Michael Cotton

God's Special Keeping

(Written for Aunty Olive Morris, nee: Downs, on Sunday 28th April 2002 at 7.35am. Mild after much needed rain overnight)

Of all the creatures of the Earth
They are not ours to keep;
Yet it should please God that we look after them
Until they go into God's special keeping . . .

He will call them to His side at will
And you must let go
And be content with the memory
And let the tears you shed be of the happy times
Recalled with your own special creature . . .

Not of the loss,
For they have not gone;
They stay with us for all time -
Only the body decays,
For the soul lives on . . .
And the spirit will come to you often.

So smile
And do not fret,
For they are with you still,
All around you
In everything that was theirs . . .

Now and then they will make it clear to you
With an unexplained gentle brush past your legs;
Or a call, so clear, in your sleep
That you wake expecting to see them . . .
And, although they are not within your sight
They are within your reach,
Always . . .

There are many helpless creatures left on Earth
Who need care and love and patience;
So tend to them in some little way,
Until they too are called to God's special keeping . . .

And in this way
God will keep a special place for you within His heart;
For He looks on at all we do and takes note . . .

Mary Pauline Winter, nee: Coleman

Choices

Isn't life just great?
Get up early, stay up late
Shall I wear red or blue?
Will it be shorts, skirt or jeans?
I'm not exactly in my teens
Shall my hair be up or down?
Will it be a smile or a frown?
Some people just survive
Some go on and thrive
Some people are all alone
Some just like to be on their own
Shall I go to the pictures or watch TV?
Maybe I'll have some company
Some people live on fantasy
I'm just glad I'm me.

E Riggott

Two Thirds Of A Year

So far, in this year, two thousand and nine
We've had the flu from the swine
The economy is in such a mess
It causes people much distress
Now house prices have risen so high
No one can really afford to buy
People grunt and people groan
Because the banks won't grant a loan
The price of food increases each week
Making the future look very bleak
Two thirds of the year has flown by
'Soon be Christmas,' I hear you sigh
Hopefully things will pick up again
And we can look forward to two thousand and ten.

Mary Shepherd

Go For It

Hello, I'm sixty-six
and precariously balance
on two sticks.
Struggle with stairs and
steps on the bus
there are plenty of elderly people like us
lightning strikes of pain in the groin
the orthopaedic surgeon said
I could join the queue for
brand new ceramic hips
enabling me to trim my toenails
and do my zips
Hip hip hooray, I can honestly say
Go for it, Go for it!
Anyway!

S K Singleton

In Sympathy

In life, in death
There is God
In times of grief
There is God
With loved ones gone
There is God
In days to come
There is God

Pray to Him
Love Him,
Believe in Him
There is God.

Susanne Humphries

Tommy

No need to wait for Tommy,
he won't be fighting back.
satisfied with spite in your eye,
that his are bruised and black.

I watched you from behind a wall,
I saw what you did.
You punched him and you kicked him,
pulled him from where he hid.

Tommy won't be running home,
no comfort waiting there,
no one to calm the terror,
no one to say they care.

Has anyone seen Tommy?
He never said a word.
His book's still wet with tearstains,
when he cried, I know you heard.

Don't hang around for Tommy,
he won't dread another day.
Lonely chair at an empty desk,
Tommy went away.

Jan Lovell

Britannia Rules The World

Many a person has signed on the dotted line,
Not knowing what they've let themselves in for.
They've joined the Army, now they go and fight
In the Iraq or Afghanistan war.
Sometimes people think it's glamorous,
Travelling around the world.
Sometimes it's an adventure,
Not realising they could be killed.
Most of them are boys and never been away from home,
They will miss their families and creature comforts,
Going on, into the unknown.
Life must be very different in hot countries,
Where temperatures rise, drinking out of polluted rivers
And no proper bed to lie.
Comrades together, brave soldiers putting their lives on the line,
Dodging gunfire and getting injured
Or maybe killed on a landmine.
The Army is their family, when they're so very far away,
But their loved ones are thinking of them
And can't wait to see them home safely one day.
Fighting for Queen and country, Britain should be so proud,
Britannia rules the world,
Are the words we should sing out loud.

Sandra Bentley

Salute To Andrew 'Freddie' Flintoff

Ashes Test 2009 and farewell to Freddie
When such a day dawns we are never ready
Guaranteed to always give his best
Fred knew that this was to be his final Test
His body has suffered for the love of his sport
There are no words to express the joy he has brought
A man who wore his heart on his sleeve
Some of his actions could not be believed
England and Lancashire through and through
Mr Cricket, such men there are only a few
A man of the people with whom many could relate
That's why Fred truly was everyone's mate
Adored and admired for his true love of cricket
Whether he was bowling or standing in front of the wicket
An innings changer, that was his role
His presence inspired when he started to bowl
The opposition knew they were in for a challenging time
The ball coming towards them in the perfect line
Stand up and be counted as he ran in
Any misjudgement at the crease and he would grin
When it came to batting he could only attack
One thing about Fred, he had courage and the knack
At times he got under the opponent's skin
The reason being he knew he could win
There's only one Fred and he will be sadly missed
Not only for cricket, remembering his antics, do you get the gist?
The reason we love him - he is human, so cheer
Life's for the living and some like the odd beer
So rejoice as we look forward to the coming one-dayers
As Fred will hopefully be selected as one of the players
Congratulations Fred and the England team for a job well done
Sunday 23rd August 2009, the Ashes were won!

Anne Sackey

Our History

Of all the places in the world
My heart is and has always been;
As in the hearts of many
In our dear England, so sweet and green.

There's not a country so very dear,
Than its sweet and gentle breeze;
That makes your heart appear to miss
A beat, with the beauty our eyes can seize.

From bluebells and primrose,
To great oak trees so tall;
Purple thistle and orchid,
Green meadows and wildlife, singing sweet calls.

From walking down an old country lane,
To the cities, it never fails to enthral,
Such sights to see wherever you are,
From wild flowers to castles, and city halls.

Our architecture is all of its own,
Such beauty it can forever instil.
The strength and power it allows you to feel,
From our craftsmen who are second to nil . . .

I wander around, completely in awe,
Of the work, done with such joy and pride;
That they could create so much beauty,
To make us aware of the passion they plied . . .

Into every brick and rock they laid,
To every bulb or seed planted with love;
And now we can see all the hard work,
Come to fruition as God intended it would . . .

For in all the Earth, whether England or other,
God plants the great seed in our minds;
To create with a passion He gave us to use,
To look at all beauty of every, single kind . . .

Janet Starkey

Untitled

Another spaghetti morning
Italian kind of day
The signpost bears a warning
That you'll be sent away
The cooker is not dirty
The plates are never clean
The landlady is quite flirty
She says she's kissed the Dean
The shop is always open
The fruit is out of date
But the people are still coping
Despite the three-month wait
The hospital has no nurses
The doctors are on strike
You can hear the patient's curses
As you walk along the dyke
Beware of imitators
Who'll try to rob you blind
They ex-Italian waiters
Who'll infiltrate your mind
So fill your car with produce
And leave this place today
Take a flask of fruit juice
To help you on your way
Go, become a German
Go and live in Bonn
Change your name to Herman
They'll never know you've gone
Then move on to Brussels
Become a Europhile
Live on soup and mussels
And live there for a while
If you go to Paris
Please mention my name
Tell them you know Harris
And you're there to shoot some game
But you'll wake up one morning
And know you must return
That spaghetti day is dawning
You mustn't let it burn

Trevor Foster

Feeling Humble

I was just a slave for you three
I moaned at my husband when he came home for tea
It's was 'fetch me this' and 'fetch me that'
I didn't have time to sit and chat
I was feeling down and ill at ease
All I wanted was a bit of peace
He looked at me, 'A change of scene it what you need.
Go and get changed, we'll go for a meal.'
We went to the best restaurant in town
I'm glad I put on my best blue gown
The meal was good, we had a drink
Then I relaxed and started to think
I glanced at the table next to ours
The young lady's husband he did look proud
He looked at his wife with adoring eyes
How pretty she was and elegant too
All of her happiness seemed to shine through
As they got up to leave he held her chair
It was then I saw it lying there
He picked it up, it was a white stick
He gave it to her rather quick
As I watched them going out of the door
I glanced at my husband, he knew what for
With tears in my eyes, I took his hand
All of a sudden I felt quite grand
Never again would I moan or grumble
Seeing that lady I felt quite humble
She was blind but she didn't grumble
She was all smiles and oh so humble
I had to sit and think for a while
All of my troubles seemed so mild
Then I realised what I wanted was right by my side.

Shirley Mather

Dance

In my dreams I can dance
By day my legs are stiff and immobile
But in my dreams I can still dance . . .

Old companions sleeping by the fire
Her little paws twitch to the rhythm of the rabbits
By day she sees and hears very little
Yet in her dreams she still chases whisker.

Our bodies are fearsome, incredibly made miracles
But when life moves to a slower phase and it will
Our minds take up the song and remind us what we once were.

God says there is a time for everything
This must be my season to be still and remember
So I won't fight this phase
Or resent the pace
Yet my mind is still free and cannot be captured
- unless I let it.

In my dreams I can dance
By day my legs are weak, ailing
But in my dreams
I dance.

Tracey Kesterton

People

There are people who do
And people who don't
People who will
And people who won't
People who help when you are in need
People who never do a good deed
There are people who take
And people who give
People who die that others may live
Good people - bad people
All colours and creed
Some who have plenty
Others in need
There are people who work
And people who play
Some people worry
Some live for today
People who laugh, people who cry
Some who are truthful
People who lie
People fight people
I want to know why
People are born
And all people die.

Lydia Barnett

The Adventures Of Curly The Hair

Curly the hair did not have a care
as he floated around the bath on a bubble
but he started to frown
as the water went down
and he found himself in so much trouble

at the end of his ride
he got stuck on the side
of the bath made of polished white enamel
he thought he could drift
and cadge a lift
on a sponge or a bit of damp flannel

so he waited and waited
and to Curly's surprise
the water level then started to rise

it made him feel happy
and with his change of luck
he cruised round the bath
on a white, plastic duck
but the water level went down again
and Curly, he made a grab for the chain
so in desperation and as we all fear
he went down the plughole and did disappear

but the point of this story
is there's no more to be said
and that Curly, the hair, did not keep his head.

Ada Pain

Soldiers

What would they have done
If they had lived their natural span?
The shining promise of their lives gone.

They went to war beneath a burning sun
That beat upon their unbowed heads.
What would they have done?

They went to war with tank and gun
Sharing and caring in comradeship.
What would they have done?

How many more will die, as they have done
Before sense prevails and all come home?
What would they have done?
The shining promise of their lives has gone.

Joan Gray

Container Ships

Storming along
Not a person in sight
Silent as snow
Wrecks scatter the ocean
Containers of wood
Thousands more of the same
Dangerous seas
Rain bashes the ship
An experienced captain
Takes us through
The cruel sea
And beyond.

Alan Hattersley

Heroes

Made by the love of two heroes
We bow down to you
Truly devoted to your work
Heroes you *never* shirk
Fairest goal in Human life
Is Human love
Heroes you fight to save
Down and above.

Nature has given you the power to save
You are brave
World's serious work must be done
You are truly the serious one.
Heroes.

Desmond Chapman

Sabbath Day

A Sabbath day of mourning, a Saturday of grief.
The happenings of yesterday are quite beyond belief.
I still can hear the shouting and the jeering of the crowd
And see the weary body beneath the cruel cross bowed.

I saw the sky grow darker and heard His final word.
I saw the Roman soldier pierce Him with his sword.
I heard Him cry, 'It's finished,' and saw the curtain torn.
I saw Him lifted from the cross and heard His mother mourn.

I saw Him buried in the tomb and watched it sealed with stone.
I saw the soldiers left on guard, then wandered off alone.
He said He'd come to save us, why did He have to die?
I cannot understand it. What is the reason? Why?

Myrtle Lucas

The Seine

The stagnant river cordons itself
With banks that rise like concrete shoulders
Hunched and inverted, harbouring France's vein

Standing above the flowerless pit
Of tramps' piss and barge fumes
I watch to see the fishes swimming

Adapted minnows with asbestos lungs
And plastic, friendly bellies could lurk
In the rusting carcass of a shopping trolley

And yet, this bridge, the Pont d'Alma
On which I stand, leads me and the swell
Of scornful onlookers to where an artist

Sits, offering, 'The Seine by night'
A darkened mass bathing irregular strokes
Of a thousand struggling colours.

Nicola Buxton

Smile Please

Bought for its fiery autumnal leaves,
the tree turned white with blossom first.
My wife bought a disposable camera
and the occasion for my portrait to be shot
against the seasonable background seemed set.
But overnight the wind and rain
seized their moment and scattered mine.

I was to have worn a short-sleeved shirt
and equally summery summer ensemble
in flowery blue, pink and green,
perpetually smiling my warmest smile.
Opportunities lost can pass in seconds
or unrecognised, take a lifetime.
Fingers crossed then for second chances.

John Younger

The Boat Race - Oxford v Cambridge

The time arrives, the hour at hand,
as Oxford and Cambridge assemble and stand,
for a race along the River Thames,
from Putney to Mortlake to find what stems.

An official toss of the sovereign on place,
to determine which side for which crew in this race,
all takes part below a blue sky,
on a warm golden day and weather so dry.

The *Blues* from bow to stroke plus cox,
position themselves prepared with their clocks,
from west side of Putney Cross,
to Hammersmith Bridge and gain without loss.

The horn is blown the race begins,
a competition to see who wins.
viewed by millions across the Earth,
the crews convey what they're worth.

Covering a distance of two miles,
during the tough and tiring trails,
a halfway mark of Surrey Bend,
the fight goes on to gain and defend.

Upon the Thames, within the walls,
come the London supporting calls,
so many thousands of folks there crowd,
as the boats come into position so proud.

Rowing past as such a pace
and showing so well a determined race,
now to aim for the three mile sign,
a fall in length to the finishing line.

So determined are the teams,
to see the cup there of their dreams,
at the point, placed to claim,
besides the bottles of champagne.

Supporting spectators seen so clear,
within the festival atmosphere,
as boats close in with moves so fine,
side by side and line in line.

The line is crossed, the moment comes,
exhausted crews of chosen chums,
such a fight to reach ahead,
as both crews now end in red.

James Stephen Thompson

Celebrations And Congratulations

Twenty-one years is a bit of a milestone
Far better of course I would say, than a millstone,
And far too early to be written on a tombstone
But Forward Press can be awarded a gemstone.
They encouraged us poets through the years by their selection
We have put pen to paper with the hope of enlarging the collection.
Brains have been exercised to bring up recollection
Bringing up words to bear to refute people's allegation.
Many themes have been penned with vigour and enthusiasm
It's a boon to yours truly laid up with rheumatism,
Ideas come thick and fast and I look forward with optimism
But I know it won't be long before hopes are dashed by opposition.
Now for twenty-one years we have gone through good times and bad
There have been great times, bad times and some have been sad.
We look to the future when successful times will be had
Although times of frustration are inclined to make us mad.
The future bodes well for the literary person
Tough times may be ours as we make our excursion,
But with fortitude and stickability we will attain our destination
The next twenty-one years will see our ramification.

John Waby

Life's Journey

The married couple have just had a child
Relations are round with presents and smiles
Isn't he sweet, the dear little chap,
But wait till he starts to crawl round the mat.

This child will grow into a man one day
Marriage? Who knows? Perhaps he may
Well he does and he's proud of his wife and kids
And the years roll by much quicker than he thinks.

His poor wife dies, now he's alone
The kids have married and all left home
But he smiles and he tries to keep going somehow
But there's not much pleasure in life for him now.

By now he's grown cantankerous and old
He can't help being grumpy and cold
Off to a home he goes, all bags packed
Very few relations pop in for a chat.

Memories are all that he has left
And to his inner self they are kept
For his short life that's left he just sits and waits
Until God decides to open the gate.

And the very next day the man's found dead
And his children come and collect round the bed
He was a very nice dad, how much money did he leave?
Was there a Will, or shares up his sleeve?

Today is the funeral, the relations flock round
Some shed a tear as they lay him in the ground
Workmen begin to cover him with earth
And on top of that goes a wreath with a verse.

With deepest sympathy to our dear dad
With love and respect from the children you had
On Earth you toiled, in Heaven you rest
God bless you Dad, you're one of the best.

N Bates

The Thirties Recalled

In nineteen-thirty or thereabouts,
Of course with dates there's always a doubt,
In the garden of Clyde House, lo and behold
Was a treat, extra special, so I was told.
It was a mini railway track
With beautiful engine, painted black.
Young Peter drove it, he's got the knack,
Eighty years on it all comes back.

A giddy scene, young driver laughing,
Adoring sister, hands a-clapping,
Father in his deckchair napping,
Mother with her neighbours chatting.

With Winston's warning voted trite,
All around seemed peace and right,
Playtime and summer bright,
Laughing children through hedgerow peeping,
Why, brookside willows, are you weeping?
We knew not then of German might
Or of that great, tremendous fight
That took so many from our sight.

Willows weeping? Well they might,
They saw the future, dark as night,
That house that knew so much gladness
Was to know the greatest sadness.

Those hands, young driver once saw clapping,
Place Christmas flowers at each year's passing,
At Derby school's war memorial,
Its hero's names there recorded
With Peter's.

George Nicklin

A Few Things Left To Try

Before I die, I want to fly
Not in a big silver plane across the sky,
Nor a loud helicopter with spinning blades,
Or even a rocket that from view soon fades.
What I had in mind was something much slower,
Like bees that drone from flower to flower.
What a glorious way to pass my time by
Yes, that's the way I want to fly.

Before I die, I want to dance,
Not a modern jig up and down kind of prance.
Nor like the Morris Country Dance with its bells
Or even a Scottish reel with hoots and yells.
What I had in mind was something with much more class,
One where a handsome boy holds his pretty lass.
Then together, they glide across the dance floor,
That's what I want and nothing more.

Before I die, I want to ride,
Not in a fast car on a motorway wide.
Nor on a bicycle trying not to fall off,
Or even a Rolls Royce like some big toff.
What I had in mind is something much more fun,
A thing that leaves you quite breathless when it's done.
To ride the Watershoot at Alton Towers,
Left on a high for hours and hours.

Just a few things left to try
Before I die.

Madge Gilbey

If Only

If only life was easy
If only life was good
So many would be happy
This I'm sure they would.
To see everyone friendly
No matter what colour or breed
Everyone could be nice
I'm sure what a wonderful world it could be.
No one would be alone
No one would be unhappy
Everyone would help another
This would be my wish
To see the world change
For the better and forever
No more war or trouble
This would make me happy
From now to ever more.

Judith Mary Drinkhill

A Maiden's Dream

Bulging muscles
Beautiful and bold
Such beauty to behold
The abs so fab
The six-pack firm to hold
Oh how beautiful to see
A body built like thee.

Robert Walker

The Dash

From date to date is life.
Time stands still for no one.
Abundance, forgiveness, loss, happiness - whatever the season
A generation, voice died out - gone.

No one to tell stories of how it used to be,
No wisdom from life to seek,
Now, not yet, never; blind can't see
Keep walking, leading, following - however weak.

Motivated by life, don't know how to live it,
The dash so small tells millions of stories
Only you know the true extent your lamp is lit
No one but you, to choose the decisions - no jury.

So what will the dash say about you?
Romantic, athletic, achiever, faithful, loyal, wise.
It's who you are not what you do,
So let go to freedom - be vulnerable; no disguise inside.

Corinne Ashton

Oh Moon

Oh moon, when we see you why is it that we all
believe that you have a face?
We just cannot understand the miracles that are
happening all around us.
When we have you in our presence
it is a great comfort when instead of being unable to see
we can feel the steely reflection of your glow.
We, through science,
have conquered the space between Earth and you,
We have been in your presence,
we are conquering space to beyond belief
perhaps to devastation.
So let's enjoy our sacred spot in this vast land of ours.

Jean Dickens

City

I see you grey, jungle dense,
Dressed in sweat-drop jewels.
Piled deep, wide and high,
Up to your ankles in stray dog stools.

Loosely wrapped in green belt,
Your high rise taken by baboons,
Whilst down below where the sun never reaches,
Dreams are popping like grey balloons.

Glass, steel, bricks and mortar,
A wedding cake of sort.
You're like a wicked, wayward daughter
Sat upon a geographical wart.

Your children are about you,
Rushing through your veins,
Bringing hot flushes to your face,
Or slowly slipping down your drains.

But it's at night that you look your best,
When your body is on fire.
I'd like to get to know you better,
In a street car named Desire.

When the pulse is racing
And all your lights are blazing green,
When all the blood spilled on the sidewalk
Has been hose-blasted clean.

A grey, chill mist of dawn
Wraps around you like a veil.
With all the night's loose endings
Still hanging from your tail.

You look at me, you took my money too,
You dumped me naked on your shore.
But like a dog who'd enjoy the licking
I turned and headed back for more.

Richard Napierski

Can't Hear The Care

I had to ring the hospital,
prayed to hear a friendly voice,
a rasping one came back to me,
I had no other choice.
Heard the absence of emotion,
just my number wanted to know,
'twas a person working a computer
where emotions cannot go.
I've come to hate the telephone.
Press this, press that, then wait awhile.
'Tis automation directing me
never a person with a smile.
Automation can't sense an upset,
don't hear a sob in the voice,
have stopped praying for someone friendly,
alas we have no choice.
Thank the Lord I can ring my friend
we can laugh and chat a while.
God forbid that technology will take this too
for my friend speaks to me with a smile.
Many people have also been programmed
Compassion is not much in view.
Many scurry for personal possessions
With values no long so true.

Rosie Hues

Baffled Of Bolton

Be an angel, pour out the elixir,
Mind the ghost, encounter an extraterrestrial,
Bump into a god,
It's all very odd having so many visitors
Whose existence we can't explain.
Have such as these leaked our whereabouts?
This little planet,
This Adam and Eve's birthplace.
Two minutes to midnight in a garden called Eden.
Are we the talk of all that's paranormal,
Of all that doesn't conform to what we call the rules of science?
Far from us being alone in the universe
An ever open door makes for
An endless stream of spectres
To pass through it.
Uninvited guests, yet at their slightest we request,
We invest in reality.
Daily I see that which isn't there
And as my chair floats in the air
I'm brought down to Earth by the thought,
Is there anybody out there?

Vann Scytere

A Mother's Prayer

My son, I've held you in my arms,
I've wiped the tears from your eyes when you hurt.
You left me when you went to school
And I sat at home and cried like a fool.
But you came home so happy and grown
And told me stories I should have known.
How could I tell you it broke my heart
To let you go into this bad world
Without me there to take your part?
My son, your schooldays are far away
Cambridge called and again you were gone.
You travelled the world as young people do
Giving to others far poorer than you.
You gave of yourself, so selfless so sure,
My son, so grown up, so very mature
You met a sweet lass with sparkling eyes,
She was your soulmate, the whole world could see.
A marriage, a wife, so happy were you
And a sweet beautiful daughter for me.
A military career pre-destined for you
Soon took precedence over all we do.
Whilst wives and mothers stay at home
Men go away, the world to roam.
Making the world more safe for some
But heartache and tears for loved ones at home.
Months go by, duties still to perform,
But news at home is happy and warm.
A baby arrived, he looks just like you
And his mother so proud, as I am of you.
Dark clouds suddenly spoil the view.
Terrorism taking its toll on you.
The war escalates, the news is not good;
Young soldiers are dying and sad to say
We were wishing you home day after day.
Then came the news we all were to dread,
A bomb had gone off and you were dead.
No happy home-coming for us or for you,
Just a broken-hearted family mourning for you.
Now the tears have all gone but the pain is still there
And so at times it will always remain,

But life goes on, as it surely should
And the time will come when we smile again.
Your wife and little boy, who looks like you,
Fill my life as you used to do.
And when I feel a little sad
I count the blessings I still have.

Elizabeth Timmins

Precious Gift

The most precious gift in life you can have
Is the love of a wonderful mother,
For I know in life that's what I had
For there could be no other.
She was always there when I needed her,
But now that she has gone,
I'm not sure how I'll cope with life,
For without her my days are long.
I miss her so much, I always will,
But now she has gone away,
I know in death she will love me
And by my side she will always stay.
Of all the blessings in this life
There's none that can compare
With the gift of a darling mother
Who would always be right there.
For without her it's hard,
But I will try to be strong,
With her as my guardian angel
I know I won't go wrong.

Lilian Bullock

The Death Camps

I feel gutted within
As if my insides are being ripped apart.
I am saddened
I am maddened
I feel sick and unable to speak
The sight before me makes me weep.

I am incensed - outraged
By man, betrayed.
The sheer insanity
The total lack of humanity.
The insane mind
That was behind this atrocity
That destroyed a race
With such ferocity.

This senseless, cold, disregard for life
To wipe out a man
His child, his wife.

The man steps into his bloody grave
Which along with his friends he has dug.
His mind void of all feeling
Tired, all belief in mankind gone.
Pitifully waiting to die
With pathetic acceptance.

The woman turns to her husband's executioners to beg.
'What have we done?
What is it you need?
I will do anything you ask,
If not for me
For the sake of my children, I plead.'

A shot - she is dead.
This is absurd!
Not a singe word of this mother
Has been heard.

The children look on
Like dirty, rag dolls.
Orphaned o' so briefly
Hand in hand they step forward
To share their fate.

Softly crying,
Harshly dying!

It is hard to understand the executioners,
Those who gave the orders.
To send, not one score, but millions
To their untimely death.

In fact I can't.

Neither can I understand the victims,
Their acceptance to die
And as for the world looking on -
Does no one hear their cry?

Do they not believe in themselves,
That they have the right to breath?
How can a man lead his family
To their own graves?
This I can't believe.

Where is the fight?
Where is the outrage?
Where did the spirit go?
At this I am saddened,
I am maddened.

I am dismayed.

Wayne Fisher

Secret World

I live in my dreams
In a sentient world,
Fuelling the rhythms of life
Whilst racing through time.
In the wink of an eye.
I live in my dreams.

I live in languorous dreams
Suffused with mellow sunshine
Streaming slowly and warmly,
Threaded with dust motes
Drowsily, gently floating
As life meanders by.

I fly in my dreams
On dragonfly wings
Dazzling and shimmering
In darting flight,
Buzz-bombing the ponds
In my woodland retreat.

I feel in my dreams
Currents of air softly breathing
While shadow dappling
The still, secret glades.
Hear plants thirstily drinking
Earth steaming after rain.

I sense in my dreams
The bluster of violent tempests
And the feathersoft touch
Of a newborn's breath
Careless winds ruffling my hair,
Tingle to the surge of the ocean's roar.

I reach out my hands
As rain cascades down
Bouncing on pavements
In shivering arcs,
Gurgling musically in gutters
Watch ballets of bobbing umbrellas.

I know in my mind the wildness of night -
The trembling call from predatory owls
Float by rose coloured clouds
On honey sweet air,
Plunge through the remoteness
Of measureless space.

I strive to remember in dreams
Echoes of lost yesterdays,
Voices and laughter
The turn of a head
And glow with the response
To loving embraces.

I store in my dreams
With the Earth in my hands,
As I stretch forth my soul
To images blurring and fading
But held fast in my heart
My treasures to plunder at will.

Linda Jennings

Ode To An Onion

You woo me with your flavour-savour skill;
Can taste buds ever hope to know your like?
Who cares, pre-prandial, that it is your will
To string along a Frenchman on a bike?

Sweet shudder-sharpness! Uncompared you stand;
And whether pickled, Spanish, spring or cooked,
You lift the lifeless and imbue the bland
With such a bite that I am hapless-hooked.

O tasty, tangy orb, you are the best -
And yet, with all your charms, 'tis surely death
When you've been busy, adding zip and zest,
To find you're boosting someone else's breath.

And I confess I do not understand
Why meeting you is hell at second-hand.

John Slim

Mahalo Hawaii

8am, solitary adventuress
walk to the beach
two miles away
such beauty, turquoise blue sea
volcanic mountains, where dragons come for their fire drink
10am return walk, it's hot
hotter than Lanka, India, Mexico . . .

I pray to reach the top of
Mapuana Street
a gentle rain begins washing away
burning, frazzled edges
just moments from my destination
blessings, Mahalo

Return to villa with pool
and seething family tension
open a treasured bottle of champagne
from the wedding couple's excess
beauty products come first over Grandmother's health
her face is plum soft and swollen
purple-blue bruises

It costs one pound twenty a minute to phone England
states the new bride wearing two hundred dollar eyelash extensions
and a shawl of greed
I down the champagne, sitting in my swimming costume
enjoying my rebellion

Later, choosing cooler times to venture out
seeking protection from mango trees
the neighbours have a pomegranate tree
further down are avocados

Lani, the Hawaiian Scottish Goddess
speaks of the Polynesian triangle
outside McDonald's
the tattoo on her ankle is a mother with several baby sharks
representing her children and grandchildren

She is seventy-five years young
with a flower in her hair
a tapestry of stories to share
Castenada mountains surround us in Kailua
I'm planning to return before
I get on the plane home
Mahalo Hawaii
Thank you.

Dorina Shannon

These Hard Times

In these hard times of no work, no pay
I manage to keep the bailiffs away.
I'm one of the lucky ones and thankful for that
Although on my budget I'll never get fat!
I can pay my mortgage, I can run my car,
I can't afford luxuries, I can't travel far.
I can't go abroad for sea and for sun,
But I don't need much money to go out and have fun.
I'm one of the lucky ones, I have friends, you see
And one in particular is closer to me.
We've seen each other through worries and woes,
We'd stand by each other against any foes.
I'm one of the lucky ones of that there's no doubt
And all of my blessings I know *and* I count.
With family and friends to help me each day
And a job I enjoy with moderate pay.
I'm one of the lucky ones and know I'll survive,
Although I'll not prosper, I *can* stay alive!

Pat Evans

I Shuffle

I shuffle
I can hear myself shuffling
When did I start to shuffle?
I never used to shuffle
Old men shuffle
Did I begin to shuffle
When I became an old man?
When was that?
When was the moment
I stopped lifting my feet
Into a stride?
When precisely?
When did the young man
Say farewell
And the old one settle down
Begin to make his home in me?
Who let him in?
It wasn't me
And where did it take place
That moment?
And why wasn't I warned
Prepared for it?
And what next?

Will I begin to smell
Decay, walk round in circles
Think small thoughts
Complain small ills
Find fault with tiny errors
Fear little fears?
And what next?

Will I forget who I am
What I've done
Achieved?
Will atrophying memory
Diminish deeds
Reduce the heart's pride?
Will the sweet past taste sour
Will I deny the child?
And what next?

Arnold Wesker

The Wood Nymph

Deep in the folds of the wood
Where trees grow close
And ferns spread their fronds
In elegant abandon

The sunlight filters through
And sheds its light in
Dappled shade
Casting shadows into nooks

Early, if you are quick
You will see the fairy
In the glory of dawn
A Venus in green silk

She stands with her hair
Draped down to her hips
Its warm, brown shades
Mingling with the tree's

Her skin white and creamy
Her breasts pert
Nipples standing erect
In the spangled light

Slender as a wisp
Legs long and lean
Feet dainty and petite
Hands slender and slim

Sunlight touches her face
Classical in its shape
Her blue eyes smile
Her lips a sensuous seduction

She drapes her body
In a wrap of green silk
And then fades into
The wood's embrace.

Carol Bradford

Sailing In No Wind

I've always hated sailing in little or no wind.
It's just like conversation with those who've never sinned.

You sit there and fret there and nothing really happens,
But the boat is slowly moving, you can see it in the battens.

You feel a little silly as the water boatmen pass.
With little dimples at each foot in water that's like glass.

You all lean on the other side to help the mainsail fill,
And the ripples round the rudder show you're very nearly still.

It's difficult to understand why you move at all,
And nowhere near exciting as sailing in a squall.

Then the wind is howling and your head is hurtling past
The frothy waves and coral heads and little bits of mast.

The helm is shouting madly that the jib is far too slack,
And you're swinging in your harness with a cruelly aching back.

The race is long with lots of tacks and some exciting gybes,
And the helm becomes excited when it's clear that we'll capsize.

The opposition's laughter hurts as they all sail quickly past.
Oh damn it! we were right up front, and now we're nearly last.

I can recommend quiet sailing in little or no wind,
Then it doesn't really matter whether or not you've sinned.

David Walter

The Cuckoo

From where did that cuckoo of golden rust come, just some far away place?
The wings were deformed like twisted girders and it could not fly,
Then dived and crashed into a nest of dry twigs, like a hunk of bronze,
The nest absorbed this hit like a syringe, drawing up some cloudy liquid.
It's a dirty hit - cut the rattling baby, it's a real hassle, know what I mean?
So the nest reverberated. Shouts, screams, then fists
Followed by social workers and police.
The nest, it always was a fragile mass of twigs, fell apart and the nestling fled,
Jumped to escape the piercing debris . . .
Gliding on a current of tangerine air which burst from the petals of a sunflower,
Yellow petals freeing themselves and carrying him higher,
Higher like a shimmer of a kingfisher, whose turquoise afterglow hangs, then evaporates like the last breath of a dying woman.
These fledglings who fly and soar become exhausted,
Reel, then spew a black phlegm and plunge.

Those who are fascinated with casualties of flight and desire to understand their beatitudes grasp the context and comprehend the sub-text, are prevented by one essential flaw:
That mass illiteracy of the literate, the language of the bourgeoisie.

Nigel Pearce

The Dark Arts

It is often said and heard
That politics is a dirty word,
The corruption, the spin
And the absurd, we note
And like the war - please don't mention the moat.

But please, spare a thought for the canvasser this time
When it comes around to election time.

Next year, Brown will be ousted for sure
But complacency is never to be
Please spare a thought for the people like me
Who will be beating a path to your door

Take it from me, it's not the best place to be.

Ringing those bells and knocking on doors
The walking the streets till your feet are sore.

Come wind, rain, or snow
Out we must go
To get out the vote once again

Election night, at the count - it's the best place to be
Pensive and pacing - the great highs and lows
Waiting to see, who stays, and who goes

The raising of glasses, the cheers and the jeers
Win, lose or draw
And the pleasant encounters from the folk at the door
Make electioneering worthwhile
I'm sure!

Mark Walker

Spring

'Walk awhile with me, dark lady,
Where the golden rushes rise;
Where the willow trees are shady
Walk awhile with me, dark lady.
With me in the woodland glady
Weave a web of loving lies.
Walk awhile with me, dark lady,
Where the golden rushes rise.'

I may go with you, bold fellow,
In the woods and by the stream.
If your irony can mellow
I may go with you, bold fellow,
Into glades arrayed with yellow:
I could realise your dream.
'I may go with you, bold fellow,
In the woods and by the stream.'

'Have my heart, you dark-haired vision:
Hear the call of spring and heed.
Hebe calls you: end suspicion.
Have my heart, you dark-haired vision.
Hearken to my soft petition,
Hasten to fulfil our need.
Have my heart, you dark-haired vision:
Hear the call of spring, and heed.'

Graham Saxby

Requiem For A Soldier

So for this old soldier the end came,
Silently, in a dim Warwickshire home.
Sound of guns long distant memory,
More distant still the insistent calls
Of bugles, lifetime ago when he volunteered
To chain himself to the Regular Army.
Behind him he leaves, on far-off fields,
Stricken bodies of deep-torn comrades.
Now he lies, funeral-wise, in church.
All around him kneel a litter of family,
Friends, old soldiers. The bugles blow
For this ultimate moment. On his coffin,
More significant than his uniform,
Is placed a cross and The Book.
Pared to essentials, take this last look
And let Christ's warrior go to his rest.

Paul Byron Norris

Jeanne D'Arc

Little more than a child she had visions of saints,
Who urged her to fight for her land.
In soldierly garb, received by the Dauphin,
She told of her love, told of her plan,
The battle was fought with an army so small,
Her wound bravely borne she almost gave all.
The Dauphin was crowned but Jeanne was ignored,
She stood apart and prayed to the Lord.
In her heart she knew that the battle was lost,
But she vowed to survive whatever the cost.
Taken by Burgundy, once more betrayed,
His own dreadful plans set to be laid.

A fire was lit in the square in Rouen,
And Jeanne died alone . . .
Her saints were long gone . . .

June Picken

To The Girls On My Retirement 1981

You put your faith in surgeons,
Who cut and carve and sew,
Their skill is pretty wonderful
As you already know.

Then the nurse is left in charge,
They are angels, nothing less,
They observe and treat each vital point,
With skill and tenderness.

I look upon them all with pride,
I see them ten feet tall,
I just stand quietly watching,
Insignificant and small.

Then I saw you, my little patient,
With a teardrop in your eye,
You gave a sweet, courageous smile
Trying bravely not to cry.

I put my arms around you,
I'd found a small important part,
A few kind words with lots of love,
Can cure a breaking heart.

I had not got the surgeon's skills,
The nurse's vital, tender care,
But when you missed your mummy's love
I was happy to be there.

My retirement is a change of life,
That money cannot measure,
The memory of courageous smiles
Are memories to treasure.

Freda Terry

Loss

Even though the rain had spluttered to a slow drizzle,
she still stood in a puddle,
a hole in her left shoe,
her socks wet through, she felt soaked,
but the mystery of hope left her desolate,
almost barren of self recognition.

The skies were brooding into melancholy,
a warm breeze blustered and threatened into fear
and a loss of redemption.
Turning away from the empty street
she caught a teardrop as it touched her lips.

Slowly she walked toward the harbour walls.
fishnets straddled the cobbled stones
and boats swayed and brushed the walls,
ropes anchored and secured, dripped as
the high tide frothed into waves washing the windows.

She let the sea spray catch the tears
and the wind whispered memories beneath the fading light,
one more step and the sea would have her,
one last glimpse of the town and a sense of loss
and then she stepped, without pause, over the edge and into the sea.

Peter Maher

The Long Goodbye

If these are the last words I'll ever say,
Ever write, or you ever hear from me,
Then I want you to know there has never been a day
When I have not thought, or cared for thee.
If I go, promise to never forget me
And never forget what we share.
Let me live on in your memory,
Because Dear Lord, the love I have for you . . . you're unaware.
As I lie here still as snow,
Makes me miss you more and more.
For darling I don't want to go,
I've never loved so much before.
My last thought as I close my eyes
And think, is you and your warm embrace.
As you talk to me I become hypnotised,
Eyes interlock, heart in the right place.
As my heart slows its beat,
I say my last goodbye.
It's hard for me to admit defeat,
Never forget me as I slowly die.

Gemma Smith

My Book - My Free Mystic Door

For many years, even though I wasn't sure why, something within me wanted to search for a mystic door,
But like I said, I did not know why or even what it was supposed to be for.
Nevertheless, from deep within I continued to search, seek and look,
But meanwhile, I began to write a certain kind of book.

Hence, even though I still wasn't sure why, I still felt that I needed a mystic door,
Yes, just somehow, I felt that I needed its lore.
Thus, for years, I carried on with my spiritual quest,
For all I could think was that it would be best.
However, I didn't really care if it was an archway, a window or even a wall with a door,
Although, within my dreams, I still seemed to know what I was looking for.

Yes, in my so very vivid dreams, it was as though I knew what it was really all about,
Yet, I dreamed so much, I could not always recall, but still I did not doubt.
But then, one day, I just looked at my trilogy, which is placed in several books,
And then I took a look at all my various poem books, that always tells in rhyme,
Yes, I have written such a lot about anything mystical, among the many lines.

Then, suddenly, I realised that a book is door-shaped and it opens and closes,
Yes, just like a door.
So, with my recognition, I then wondered if my mystic door has been there since I began to actually write.
For within the stories, etc. there is a heck of a lot of philosophy and prophecy,
Yes, more than enough to show me a light.

Thus with taking all that into consideration,
I thought for some time, but then came to a realisation,
For I knew that in most of my stories and many of my poems, they are about the mystical side of life,
Yes I did that many times, for it definitely helps me to get rid of strife.
Thus with that understanding, I asked myself several questions
And came to the conclusion that I'm likely right,
For usually when one does search for anything, it's often straight in front, so actually in sight.

So like my title for this verse, am I right?
Yes, was it in front of me all this time?
For after all, it was in my story and also in my rhymes.
Thus if I am correct, I'm sure that it's more than high time I found myself a mystic door,

Yes, that must be true, as I don't want any more doubt and of that I'm positively sure.

So just maybe, I needed some mystic glasses to find my mystical door,
But now that I know where it is, I certainly know what it is for.
As in my story and in many of my rhymes there is both mystical and spiritual philosophy,
Yes plain enough to see.
Thus again, straight in front of me and from me, so no charge to enter the door,
For since I'd written it all, it was entirely and utterly free.
Yes true, so just maybe I was once again given some inspired inspiration, so I was able to see more clearly,
I hope that's true, as now that I've been made aware I'm sure there should be much more cheer.

Rhowen-Margot Brown

2100 Oddity Three

I stand in Harborough Square
I gaze at the shops there and then
In the middle of Harborough Square
Is a rocket on wheels, all ten!

People getting onto the 'rocket'
Thinking it's only a ride
Where side to side the stationary 'rocket'
Pretends to fly though space and tide.

But this 2100
And the rocket is very real
But I got myself aboard
For just £5.40, what a deal!

The door closes on Harborough Square
And opens again on a different world
Red buildings, orange sky, orange grass
And friendly, blue-skinned people, yellow hair curled.

H Griffiths

My Garden

Out in my garden are memories fair
And it's always pleasant to linger there.
The birds come to visit it every day
And my reward is their song and play.

The grass is green and the flowers are bright
And each of the seasons is pure delight.
As gifts from my friends are planted here
And are thought of often throughout the year.

Some plants remind me of far off days
Of friends who have left and gone their ways
And of friends who are no longer here
But are recalled with love and a silent tear.

And here in my garden, under blossom of pear
There is a gravestone lying there;
As I gaze down I can hear again
The joyous bark of my faithful Ben.

Out in the garden, amongst the trees
I often linger with my memories.
Most brought to life in my garden there
By a few small plants people come to share.

So take care of your garden and you will find
That the plants and the friends are intertwined
And the cutting you shared some time ago
Like the friendships then will blossom and grow.

Lorraine Bosworth

The Lake Of Serenity

The early morning mist enshrouds
The lake in spectral, mystic mood.
The intertwining, swirling clouds
Create a haunting interlude
In which the soul is lulled to peace,
And present turmoils clam and fade
As inner tribulations cease,
And worries safe to rest are laid.

Now as the mist begins to rise,
The lake becomes reflective, clear.
And nature's beauty greets the eyes,
As overhanging trees appear.
The sunbeams dance upon the lake,
And birds sing high up in the trees.
They swoop, refreshing sips to take,
Then soar, to glide in morn's fresh breeze.

With them my heart in rapture soars
Above the lake, above the trees,
To revel in a blissful pause,
And irksome stress and strain release.
The lake now gleams with heav'nly hue,
Its rippling wavelets frisk with glee,
Inspiring sweet content anew
In one who sought serenity.

Eileen Nancy Blackmore

Aimee

They placed her in my arms
I beheld her face, so familiar
and loved beyond all meaning,
how my arms have ached for
so long to touch those tiny
fingers as they curl around my own.

My baby looks at me and knows
my face, for I am her and
she is me, we are one, part
of the same, incomplete when
apart. The look which passes
between us says it all,
'Hello Mum, I'm home.'

The emptiness which has been
with me, disappears, you are
here my.Aimee my beloved
how I love you.

An angel, so perfect in every
way, with eyes that melt your
heart and a smile to light the world.

How lucky I am to know
happiness such as this, and I
Pray from the depths of my
soul, 'Thank You Lord, for
another miracle - the birth of
my second daughter.'

May wisdom light your way
and happiness fill your days
and love be your constant
companion, my Aimee.

Carol Bartram

The Seedling

They planted me a while ago,
Waited patiently for me to grow,
I held my head up to the sky
And waved about as they walked by.
'Feed me please,' I whispered to them,
'Then I'll grow, don't ask me when.'
A plastic bottle held over my head,
Two capfuls in and little said.
My little body forged forward now,
Three more leaves, I gave a bow.
With gentle care, protection and love!
That's all I need, a little shove.
A seedling gone, a plant mature,
They loved me so of that I'm sure.
But soon they'll be a seedling new,
I'll lose my looks and I'll be through!

Elizabeth Corr

A Spark Of Tenderness

Cycling homewards, along a tree-lined avenue
A very strong wind blew against all and sundry,
I notices a small, delicate brown leaf leave the branch of the mother tree,
The wind shifted it rapidly towards the ground,
It rose up again, so light, so frail.
Then landed graceful to join a host of other fallen leaves
Just an incident in time, in season;
Autumn to be precise.
An unexpected spark of tenderness rose in my heart,
Seeing the nature of that fall, feeling somehow the grace.
The leaf will eventually form dust,
The resulting dust will probably dance everywhere, borne again
By the wind.
It may even seek my nostrils before joining the rich, brown soil
Of Mother Earth, giving new life to the scared roots of Nature's trees.

This recycle of Nature, so sacred in its duty,
Holds me eternally in its thrall.

Liz Cameron

Traveller

I am what life made me
And only life can change
Let no one else forbade me
Only life can rearrange
And as I have travelled along
This sometimes, a lonely road
It was only when I was wrong
So much heavier was my load
Even through the darkest day
God, He became my light
Always there to show the way
And His way was always right
All along the way
The happiness that I have shared
It was God above that did repay
With a love that can't be compared
Now as this long and winding road
Is slowly coming to the end
God above, He was my highway code
My Saviour and my friend.

Jeff Hobson

Sir John's Farewell

The Old Warren Arms they have started
To demolish today, Stapleford folks should
Have made a fuss and had their say, one of
The last old buildings in the town, not many
Left, all pulled down, the old manor went
Years ago, how they got permission I
Do not know,

The pub took the Warren's family name
And Sir John's coat of arms, with motto
(Not for me, but for God and King)
A few years time all forgotten, such
A shame, a coaching inn many years ago
On the Derby to Nottingham road, the
Warren the travellers all did know.

The Government's Statutory Adviser says
No historic interest, so Stapleford will have
To let it rest, the town grew up around the
Warren, take out the heart, but they think
They know the best.

Anthony Hull

Birthdays

If you have a birthday
And still feel very young,
Just keep that special feeling
As you keep travelling on.

For there is a popular saying,
You are as old as you feel.
So keep praying then God will help you
To realise you have a good deal.

That He will help you to keep going
And enable you to do so many things,
So all you need is to try your best
With the pleasure that it brings.

But sometimes if you do feel older
Than the age you really are,
He can give you the strength to get over it
And go back to the way you were.

Iris Covell

Dawn

The piercing sunlight shines its third degree,
A well aimed elbow activates the spouse.
Barefoot, a zombie treads the bathroom trail,
Scarce time to breathe before it leaves the house.

And so it happens every working day,
The ceaseless struggle getting up each morn,
Declaring that, when holidays come 'round,
We'll lie abed and never see the dawn!

A different story when we have the chance!
Instead of resting, out of bed we leap,
With eyes as crystal clear and mind alert,
The body now incapable of sleep.

Psychologists could doubtlessly expose,
With high-flown words and explanations deep,
The perverse trick that nature plays on us
That makes us rise, when we have the chance to sleep!

Ted Hancock

Some Holiday

Holiday brochures by the score
Scattered over the parlour floor,
Oft perused a thousand pages,
Oft times spent many weeks of wages.
Shall we go to the Antipodes
Or just up the way to Stockton-on-Tees?
Or shall we go to Timbuktu?
Please, somebody, tell us what to do.
Do you think we'll appear neurotic
If we choose somewhere exotic?
How about a holiday cruise
With plenty to eat and lots of booze?
Perhaps after all to sunny Spain,
There to escape the wind and rain.

Now that was all many moons ago
And here we are, all ready to go.
No valid passports, no traveller's cheques,
No aeroplanes, no rolling decks.
We are going just two streets away,
The painters are moving in here today.
We'll be on hand in case we're needed,
All their problems can then be heeded.

Percy Walton

21 Today 2009

We are proud to be the largest publisher of poetry in the world
Every book published by Forward Press is sent to
Libraries, creating records of every poem we have published.
Now we have come of age,
To mark this achievement we must celebrate
Yes, we think of the love on each page
Forward Press, the people's publisher
I am proud to have a poem in nine books
So let's submit a poem to be considered for publication,
The special series of Regional Anthologies for 2009.

Vera May Waterworth

Autumn Tints

Thank you, God, for making blue,
Cloudless, endless, arching skies
Meet the sparkling, azure sea
Where the wide horizon lies.

Thank you, God, for making gold
Sun-warmed sand beneath the feet.
Sunflowers by old cottage doors,
Rolling harvest fields of wheat.

Thank you, God, for making red,
Flaming sunsets all ablaze
Bright hips and haws in hedgerows grow,
To feed the birds on winter days.

Thank you, God, for making green,
Dappled shadows, ivied walls,
Tall, leafy trees and shady lanes,
On velvet lawns God's blessing falls.

Betty Maureen Rollitt

Levavl Oculos

I lift my eyes, like David, to the hills
to where the sun rejoices in the east.
His glory glows before Him,
till it fills and overflows the horizon. Like a priest
the tower at Broadway lifts adoring arms
within the encircling fire. I lift my heart
and echo words of worship from the Psalms
and sing aloud, 'O Lord, how great Thou art!'

Later I lift my eyes in awe again
to where, beyond the willow in the west
the circuit of the Bridegroom ends, and when
His splendour sinks below the Malverns' crest
and amethyst and crimson lustres dim,
the moon and stars take up the eternal hymn.

Marguerite Kendrick

Not Forgiven

I'm so lonely, I'm sad and I miss you
Now you have left and you're gone without trace.
How it hurts deep inside I can't tell you,
But you would know if you looked at my face.

No one knows how I hurt and I yearn, dear
Long to be near you and hold you again,
How I knew you would go and would leave here
But I could not have imagined the pain.

Now you're gone from my life it's for always,
Though I smell your fragrance still on my skin,
You care not in your act of betrayal,
How I feel now you've committed this sin.

Like a knife through the heart, without reason
What possessed you to inflict so much pain?
No, I don't require your explanation
I know it's over, the end of the game.

Though I love you, that goes without saying,
Yes and still need you; I have from the start,
But an end to this pain I am praying
Now we're just ships in the night, swept apart.

Like that bolt from the blue at our meeting,
How our lives changed, now they change once again,
Couldn't have known our love was just fleeting,
Angel now gone, but the demons remain.

Not forgiven, you've broken my heart.

Janet Emery

My Sister Mary

Mary was two years older than I
She was tall, slim, like Mother
I myself was short like Dad
As young girls we didn't always agree
Especially at bedtime
It was, 'You've got all the clothes!'
And 'You've got all the room!'
We shared, washing up, one wash, one dry
Mother was very good at dressmaking
Only she made us one each
Not always the same colour
I myself ended up with two
When Mary outgrew hers
Mother gave us both a Bible one Christmas
Also we both received bicycles on our 14th birthdays
Years passed, as teenagers we grew
At 17 years and 19 years Mary was nursing, I a confectioner
And bridesmaids we became to our elder brother
Again, Mother made our beautiful,
cornflower-blue figured satin dresses, with Alice bands of flowers to match
We felt so proud, looking lovely that August day
Handiwork of Mother
All so long ago.
Two years later Mary was 21,
I myself, coming 19 years, quite handy with icing ability decorated her 21st
birthday cake, made of course by Mother
Although our paths have severed
Memories last forever
Have a lovely 80th birthday Mary, in December!

Irene Grace Corbett

Over In Seconds

I heard the commotion -
things falling about,
I looked over the fence
as a dog bolted out
from the back of the bungalow
of our neighbours' next door;
he seemed in a hurry
to get to the lawn.

'Twas then I saw the rabbits,
O, why were they there?
'Run rabbit, run,' I cried,
'hide, hide, hide,' but where?
They just sat there, motionless
with no sign of alarm
as the dog bounded past them -
he would do them no harm.
For he knew all about them -
rock hard, couldn't run if they tried.

The dog, a regular visitor,
may have just arrived in a car,
and being keen to stretch his legs
headed straight to the lawn.
He may have knocked things over
in his haste to get going.
Hence the commotion, over in seconds.

John Keyse

Snowdonia To The Welsh Coast

Travel the road, a rocky ledge
Sculpted in the mountain's edge,
To slopes whereon the mosses grow
And deep green valleys sleep below.

Follow the track where plateaux drift
And stirring breezes' fingers sift
To buffet grass and toss the air
And comb our moisted, mist-damped hair.

Where bracken trampled, not by man
Ever since the world began,
Protects the rambling, rough wooled sheep
And countless creatures safely keep.

Soon the mountains greyly rise,
Stretching upward to the skies,
Leave behind the plain and fell,
For heavenly heights where red kites dwell.

Up and on but to descend,
Till we reach our journey's end,
Where pebbles usurp the rocks and turf,
To etch the tracks of swirling surf.

Gulls strut the shell-strewn hardened strand,
To parade and search that rippled sand
Left by the ebbing seas in scorn,
Until the shore once more is born.

Ann Keenleyside

My Eden

As I walk through my small garden
One warm, fine spring day
Blue skies above, not a cloud to be seen
The violet, primrose and snowdrops
Are over and gone.
But the daffodils and bluebells dance
In the sun.

The perfume from the lilac filters through.
Yellow iris stand so stately and tall
As the poppy and pansy show off their pretty faces
While the old dog rose peeks through the arch
Jasmine and sycamore are doing fine
But I must not forget the forget-me-not.

The smell of rosemary and thyme
As you brush past
While the roses grow by the side of the lawn
White jasmine grows over my front door
I do love my garden
It's my Eden
My tiny bit of paradise.

Hazel McMullan

The Birth Of A Daughter

The birth of a daughter
Is very, very special
to the Mother who bore her,
the most precious gift of all.
She should love and adore her,
Protect her whenever she can.
She should starve if need be
To feed and clothe her.
She should kiss and cuddle her,
Talk and sing to her,
Sat upon her knee.
She should wash and bathe her,
Tend to her little needs.
She should teach her about Jesus,
Protect her from evil,
Teach her how to pray and forgive,
To prepare her for the outside world.
Ready for the day she herself gives birth.
Then she will know,
She has given her daughter
The most precious gift of all.
How to love and be loved,
Then pass this love to her child.

Lorraine Haslam

Fire, Earth, Air And Water

A blistering heat, furious furnace,
Ravenous fire;
A noble spire
An evergreen path to Heaven
In flames fallen,
A pillar, beacon, bearer of hope
Now stretched out
In total submission.
Strength and girth
Shrinking and sinking.
Slow flames licking
The last bloom of birth.
Embers glowing, singeing and singing
Their death knell,
Consuming, consuming.

In the smouldering embers
Hardly a glow remains.
The solitary shape almost groans
As it slips on its side
Charred and misshapen.
Still not sufficiently far from destruction.
The breeze whispers, 'Will you reawaken?'

Nothing more
Grey ashes sigh,
In stillness cry
'All is said, Thy will be done.'

And will lives on;
A silent wind moves mysteriously,
Handfuls of charcoal dust escape
Dropping gently on leaf mould.
Beating rain takes hold,
Embedded leaves sink deeper into activity
Of perpetual decay and transformation.
A living tomb,
Protective womb
And life of a future generation.

Alison Hodge

The One That Got Away

I feel I have to write
And ode to the humble pea.
I don't know of anyone else
Who reveres the pea like me.
It makes me laugh, it makes me cry,
Why on Earth? you say
Well, here goes,
I'll try my best to tell you why -

Love them or hate them
They're a sight to behold,
Small, round, green,
Millions are sold
To unsuspecting customers around the world.
How do you catch them
When they're rolling around the plate
Or try to find them
When on the floor they decide to wait?
Until a few months later, there it is!
I've found it squashed, what a sin.

Yet another delightful pea
Will end up in the bin
I was in the supermarket once
At the frozen vegetable freezer
I took out a packet of peas
When by my side was an elderly geezer
He said, 'You'd better watch those.'
I said, 'Why? What's wrong with those you bought?'
He replied, 'When I got them home
I found there was one pea short!'
How does one eat peas?
Using a fork gives a lot of strife
Unless you use a spoon
Many people eat them with a knife.
I'd better end this sorry tale
About my favourite veg - the pea
I've just one more comment to make
Wherever you be, let your pea go free!

Christine M Powell

Edgehill - October 1641

Prince Rupert had his cavalry,
Tried in battle and the darling of the Rhineland,
Stood on the heights, on that fateful Sunday in 1641.
He begged his uncle, King Charles I,
To let him attack the rebels in the valley below.
He was confident of routing the enemy.
Charles I gave the order and so
The Civil War began.

The Parliamentarian horse were mostly farmers
On cart horses. It seemed nothing could stop
The Royalist charge.

When they got to Kineton,
They searched for booty in the baggage trains,
And looked for farmers' daughters to rape.
Prince Rupert did not order them to regroup
And go back to the battlefield, thus
Precious time was lost.
He let his men have some sport.

Meanwhile, an obscure captain
Called Oliver Cromwell,
With a small group of Cavalry,
Charged the Royalist foot . . .
They fell to the sword like stubble.

Fighting far into the night,
Both sides claimed victory.
Finally, the king relinquished the heights
And made his HQ in Oxford.

Cromwell was not satisfied,
He wrote to John Hampden,
Requesting permission to forge the New Model Army,
With cavalry called the Ironsides.
To deal with *'these gentlemen of honour'*
As Cromwell contemptuously called them.
The New Noodle Army was the Royalist quip,
They never lost a battle - Marston Moor,
Naseby, and defeated the Scots at Preston.

In spite of Charles II restoration in 1660,
Parliamentary democracy was here to stay.

Edgehill left 1500 dead, and a host of wounded.
Both sides were tended by Parliamentarian women
From the village of Kineton.
A sharp frost that night was a boon,
It sealed the wounds.

Now, ironically,
An army camp of pioneers occupy the valley below Edgehill,
They guard the H bomb
Which is kept in a bunker outside Kineton.

Edgehill is now a verdant woodland
And grassland and the steep slope,
And just past the brow,
Stands the village of Radway,
Where bullet holes can still be seen in the ancient church door,
To remind us of terrible events
All those years ago.

R O'Shaughnessy

Starlight

O mighty moon, fabled enchantress thou,
Whose smile alights upon the realms below,
What visions meet your cool celestial gaze
Through star-crossed lovers' dark, benighted ways?
The lean-faced prisoner shackled to his woe,
Palms his murderous hands and stilly prays
With silver sighs that ape the sun's spent rays.
Sorrowful soul-beams spreading through the night
Illude the long dead thing that cast their light
Like stars that live no more but only shine
In ghostly echoes, echoing through time.
Mankind's imprimatur is stamped forthright,
Conveying noble parts throughout the line -
And Brother Death's forgiven of his crime.

Paul Thompson

Compensagion

I'm getting old; it's really rather fun.
There's lots to do before my day is done.
I am not worried yet by the thought of death
There is no shortage yet of breath.
The hand now writing is unwrinkled still,
Bodily functions are controlled by will.
What is the symbol then of gathering age
In what way have I climbed another stage?
Quite simple; I can now with ease recall
People, events and places which have all
Laid dormant though the active of my days
And now return; for memory has ways
To throw back twenty years and there, a face,
Or forty years - quite clear, a darling place.
Feel still the grief at anger of rejection
Capture the anguish in a deep dejection
And smile and say how very, very young
But listen, objective, to the song as sung.
Experience it crystal clear and dear
Avoid the void of years but very near;
Reflective now, though still in life engaging,
I realise how life is compensaging.

Peter Wallace

Thoughts From Abroad

I'm homesick for those distant hills,
The blue-remembered hills,
To see once more above the plain,
Their shoulders set against the sky.

I see the blue high blade lie
Sharp and clear, yet they rise,
Where the skylark sings
Over vales, church bells may ring.

Above, clouds drift and meet,
Where jagged rocks provide a seat,
The land below is slung
Like some inverted bow.

I hear a sound that's high and low,
Within my heart begins to cry,
I'm homesick for those hills,
Those dear blue remembered hills.

Beyond those tall and pointed spires
Where anxious blackbirds call,
They firmly stand like Roman walls,
Those blue remembered hills.

Roderick Scorgie

Battle Of Bosworth Field

August 1485, Richard III on Bosworth died
Plantaganets of York on banner borne
By Shakespeare in history scorned.
On horseback led his armoured knights
Last English king from fore to fight.
With coat of arms on shield did charge
Into the midst of warring mass.
Later, on that savage day
He crashed to ground from dead mount dazed,
'My kingdom for a horse,' did shout
as overwhelmed by Richmond's might.
The House of Lancaster victory won
Henry VII's reign begun.
Wars of the Roses now at end
Into Tudor Dynasty England Blends,
With Hastings of 1066
And Battle of Britain and the Blitz
Bosworth Field in importance fits.
In splendour of Leicestershire countryside
A feast awaits enquiring minds.

Robert Fallon

21 Today

The days have gone by
So quickly
Just can't believe it's true
That we will be
Celebrating
Your 21st with you!
Get out the flute glasses
'Pop' the champagne
Enjoy every bit
Make the memories remain.

Tina Hall

Pink Elephants - And Flat Champagne

'Come up to my room,' he said
'And see my etchings,' he said
The spark he had planted
Like lightning in my eyes
My mouth tasting oysters
And champagne bubbles
As an orchestra of cellos
Led me to his log-fired room
The etchings of pink elephants
Having all of his undivided attention
As the champagnes bubbles burst
And the orchestra fell flat
While he offered me fishpaste sandwiches
And turned off the central heating . . .

Pauline Christina Knight

Loughborough November Fair

I cast my mind back to 1948
as our yearly fair did create
a powerful magnet of joy and delight
the bright lights, noise and smells too.

It was a hive of dodgems
coconut shies and spinning, whizzing machines
that gave me a scare.
The helter skelter and candyfloss
is more my style,
and to clutch at Grandma's arm
and scurry off home in the dark.

But after moving night
the streets all quiet, bare and clean
you wouldn't know that
our 700 year old fair had been.

Mary Wain

Till Tomorrow

My life was quiet, so dull and void,
Till I found something of which I'm proud.
Was enrolled at college with my work of employ,
To learn more and widen anew
Things I'd forgotten from yesterday's few.
The first day of term, with students so young,
With me, a married mum with four,
Was that of panic, apprehension so borne,
But soon came aloft with someone I knew.
We talked and time passed until Tutor arrived,
Were shown to our classroom, where we spent all day
And soon were introduced to people, all new,
From all walks of life they came, just like me,
To widen their knowledge in the work that they do.
Panic, apprehension, all soon were gone,
Our interest enlightened as the day wore on,
Each lesson, each teacher, was something new,
Baffling at times but very interesting too.
We all meet each Thursday for the next year,
What knowledge we can learn if we try hard,
From teachers with wisdom far greater than ours,
The end of the day drew sadly to its close,
With friends I had made we went through the doors
Of the college which was now a gift to us all.

B Reeve

Aunt Floss, Uncle Dan Bohane

(Dedicated with much love forever to Aunt Floss and Uncle Dan in Heaven)

In Birmingham's, Ladywood Galton Tower Block,
Flat number fifty four,
Aunt Floss, Uncle Dan how do I express
My love, being there with you alone?
In Birmingham's, Ladywood Galton Tower Block,
Flat number fifty four,

In Birmingham's, Ladywood Galton Tower Block,
Flat number fifty four,
Sitting quietly, without a word,
You would listen to all my problems,
In Birmingham's, Ladywood Galton Tower Block,
Flat number fifty four,

In Birmingham's, Ladywood Galton Tower Block,
Flat number fifty four,
Then advise me.
I miss you so much,
How do I express the love I feel
For Aunt Floss and Uncle Dan forever,
Now you have gone to Heaven?
In Birmingham's, Ladywood Galton Tower Block,
Flat number fifty four.

Edmund St George Mooney

My Son's Wedding

As Christmas approached of 2008
Steven knew he could not wait
To ask Rachel to be in his life
To share his home and be his wife
He bought the ring, hid it away
Hoped she'd say yes on the big day
Imagined the smile upon her face
As he did so his heart would race
He arranged a meeting with her dad
Would he be happy, would he be sad?
I have a huge question that affects my life
I want to ask Rachel to be my wife
As you are her father, I ask for her hand
I want to give her a wedding band
Andy beamed and the answer was yes
It's to be a surprise so don't let her guess
Steven asked Rachel to be his bride
Heart full to bursting, filled with pride
Summoned his courage, got down on one knee
Said, 'Rachel, I love you, will you marry me?'
She stood right in front of him, beamed with pride
'Yes, Steven, I'll marry you, be your bride.'
Ring on her finger Rachel danced round the room
Was that her heart going *boom, boom, boom?*
Christmas morning of 2008
Neither of them would forget that date
Now here we are in 2010
This day seemed so far away back then
Rachel looks beautiful, a stunning bride
Here we all stand, so full of pride
Steven looks handsome, so happy today
Did her dad shed a tear when he gave her away?
This day starts the rest of their life
The day that Steven made Rachel his wife.

Christine Hawthorne

Our Wonderful World

To look at pictures of time long ago,
Earth before man, back to nature we go.
Imagine the sights the eyes would take in,
Nothing to spoil the beauty within.

No buildings or factories, polluting the air,
Just wilderness left without any care.
Flowers and insects, fish in the sea,
Even small animals running quite free.

The stories we read, not sure if they're right,
Of earth way back then and what was her plight.
Dinosaurs made it their home we all know,
Fossils were found, now in museums for show.

Then arrived humans; trouble begins,
The start of the fighting, beginning of sins.
How did we happen? The theories are vast,
The question to ponder - how long will we last?

The Garden of Eden for the biblical mind,
Of Adam and Eve and the apple they find.
Scientists differ in thought, as you know,
Descendants of apes, do you think this is so?

Just look at the ocean, that vast scenic view,
The stories of earth, I think they are true.
There still are dense forests and tribes living free,
No car to the office or television to see.

Antarctic and poles are covered with ice,
I bet before man it still looked as nice.
Are we here for a reason? I'm wondering why,
Let's hope to protect earth, we really should try.

Our earth is quite lovely, whoever we are,
But don't forget space, each interesting star.
Are there some others who think as we do?
They may send a message and give us a clue.

After we leave our sweet Mother behind,
Another strange mystery, not sure what we'll find.
Do our souls start again and recycle around,
Thus returning to Mother Earth, back from the ground?

Betty Hattersley

Summer Showers

Sing me songs of summer showers
Sand and shingle hot 'neath feet
Sing me songs of seagulls' cry
Evoking memories sharp and sweet.

Crystal beads from summer's blue sky
Darker splashes on the sand
Soft and cool on upturned faces
Gentle on my outstretched hand.

Sing me songs of summer showers
Sing me of the swelling tide
Running quickly up our beaches
Where the seagulls swooped and cried.

Sing to me of long lost playmates
Sing of days of joyous hours
Sing of lovers strolling, sighing
Sing me songs of summer showers.

Frances Marie Cecelia Harvey

21 Congratulations

lift your glass, you've come of age.
Thousands of poets will celebrate same.
Dear Poet! I was so proud to read,
This title I felt weak at the knees.
I wrote a poem many years ago
From then well, poems began to flow.
I've written about the wars;
Subjects so many, moon, sky, rain and waterfalls.
You've set my brain in quite a whirl.
I've written poems about girls and boys,
I've had people ask if I could write a poem for them.
You've made me so proud, yes my brain does roam,
I have put my poems into songs.
37 in total, this can't be wrong,
Thank you for making me a poet and songwriter.

Derrick Bright

Cromford Canal - The Sleeping Beauty

Historic, lovely waterway
to stir imagination,
it is our wish to waken her -
a lovely navigation,
from Cromford Wharf to Buckland Hollow
she stretches her lithe limbs
just like a nude by Titian
and one the master wins.

Exemplary, her secular form
and figure so sublime -
extend their reach to Langley Mill
and Pinxton colliery mine,
the Erewash and Portland Basin
are her golden source -
a Mecca and a pilgrimage
for tourists to set course.

We must restore her bridges, tunnels,
lovely locks and wharves,
her branches and her culverts
red and black with subtle mauves,
a spring clean for her networks
and the Lea Wood Aqueduct
and a brush for all her fretworks
just as Arkwright might instruct.

Through aqueduct, bridge and tunnel
her beauty with us still,
until the age of steam's iron funnel
and obdurare to iron will;
it is our wish to awaken her -
in fact our moral duty,
to see her dance with wildlife scenes
the noble Sleeping Beauty.

Kenneth Berry

Thunderstorm

The cherry tree acted as a beautiful canopy
against the heat of the sun.
The cheery blossom fluttered majestically as it fell by my feet.
Creating a white, fragrant carpet of sweet-smelling blossom.
One could almost doze in its hypnotic aroma.

The day was hot and humid
And, as the sun shone the sky began to take on a darker hue.
A slight breeze began to make its welcome presence in the humidity,
The sky blackened and the gentle breeze began to pick up ferocity,
As a flash of lightning lit up the now dark sky.

Trees began to sway, gently at first,
Then with a renewed vigour they swayed to an almost violent degree.
Their branches creaked and groaned,
The trunks almost appearing to move,
as if the trees would topple over at any moment.

Leaves suddenly flew in a wildlike manner,
As if caught in a whirlpool, as the wind whipped the leaves into a
Dancing frenzy on the ground.

A spot of rain fell, followed by huge droplets,
It appeared as if someone was counting the raindrops
By size and time, each one individually.
The fall of the rain had begun to pick up speed.
In an instant the heavens had opened,
And the water cascaded downwards
As if a waterfall had suddenly changed direction.

Lightning flashed and thunder roared.
Thor, the god of war, was making his presence felt again
in the heavens.
The thunder seeming to rock the very foundations
of trees and buildings.

The sky began to brighten,
Patches of blue became more prominent against
The black, storm-laden sky.
The wind began to drop and slowly the rain eased.

A rainbow stretched across the sky,
Its colours shimmered in the dulled sunlight,
That slowly started to creep out again.

The sun spread its brilliant rays in a wider circle,
The ground began to steam as vapour rose to meet
The heat of the sun.
Rain droplets fell from the trees,
Making a splash on the now almost dried ground.

Birds began to sing again as they flew to the ground,
Their feathers wet and bedraggled,
Shaking their feathers they began to chirp loudly,
As they feed on the abundance of insects,
The insects forced up out of the soil by the torrential rain.

The sun was almost at its brilliance once again
And of the storm there was no trace
Except for the flowers,
Whose faces seemed to have taken on a more radiant glow
In their abundance of colours.

Alas! my cherry tree appeared to have lost some of its canopy,
For its blossoms lay in disarray at my feet,
A soggy mess,
My beautiful carpet of blossom was no more.

Fliss Edwards

Secrets - Oil Painting By John Dann

Who turned the key, who laid bare
The precious secrets lying there?
Who gave the rose?
Against whose warm neck did those pearls gently glow?
Dare I peer into the casket
Take a letter, slyly read it?
What will it be?
A lover's tryst or sad farewell?
I will not pry, I will not tell
I will not steal the artist's secret
I'll just keep the memory of it.

Brenda Dove

A Bonnie Shaljean Concert

Surrounded by the darkness of the room
I sat, spellbound, amidst expectant throng
And gazed on you, on whom the yellow bloom
Of seven candles shone, the evening long.
You then, with fingers skilled, addressed the strings,
And music rippled through the still dark air,
Uplifting hearts, like nightingale that sings,
You and your harp, an entertaining pair,
And as the night progressed, sweet music flowed
Like sparkling water from eternal spring,
Washing the minds of those whose faces glowed
With happiness, at hearing your harp sing.
An evening of music from the past,
In many minds forever it will last.

Leslie Salmen

Time For Celebrating

It's time to have a party
Let's give those guys a hand
We can't celebrate without music
So come, strike up that band
Forward Press has come of age
Reaching the age of twenty-one
Something worth celebrating
So come and join in everyone
Helping poets, both near and far
As I'm sure you get the hint
Publishing many anthologies
Authors get to see their work in print
Twenty-one years is a milestone
An achievement nonetheless
So I offer, with great sincerity
Congratulations to Forward Press.

Janet Hughes

Where Were You God?

tissue life
torn by politics.
Where were you God
when the bloody arm
slapped the pavement hard,
when curdling screams
crawled the tunnel walls
and guts spread like butter
on a day that barely yawned?
Where were you God
when the detonator
took him to his nirvana
and left behind the stink of fear?
What are we
but worthless bits of paper
to be discarded at will?
The futility of the daily grind
maps out a bloody butcher's yard.
Where were you God
when the papers
were left unread,
when daily words
were left unsaid,
when drink
never reached the lip
and the pen never traced a line?
What do we say to children's cries?
The tiger savaged lambs
with his breath and hungry eyes?
Where were you God when the lights went out?

Carole Payne

A Fateful Day In February

The day was dark, sombre and grim.
The inside of the house seemed brooding,
The light could not get penetrate form outside to within.
Depression was rife, as if anticipating death and strife.
The afternoon light faded and twilight filtered in,
I sat alone in the gloomy living room.
The TV I had turned on - excitement had come at last.
I watched a rugby match, a fight, a struggle,
England and the Springboks.
I was absorbed, depression lifted as I watched the players gifted.
The telephone rang, 'God,' I said, 'who could that be,
Who the Hell on Saturday wanted me.'
A voice I knew at the other end, I knew quite well,
It was my mother I said, 'What the Hell,'
'Your father's gone, I do not know where to look.'
'Phoning me will not get you off the hook.'
My wife·said, 'It doesn't sound good to me,
I think you should go, if only to see'.
I got into my car and thought, *well, it is not far to go,*
I pulled into the drive and parked my car,
Opened the gate, it was not very far.
The door of the outhouse I opened wide,
What I saw was not real, but it was inside.
Hanging from a beam, his toes touching the ground,
Was the body of my father.
His face was contorted, he was not at peace.
A knife I fetched and cut him down,
Like a rag doll he fell to the ground.
I propped him up against the wall.
My mother in the bedroom was hiding,
She could not cope, she did not know what to do.
Why me, I thought, *why should I be committed*
When the person next to him was not fitted?
I did the jobs that had to be done,
Inquests and funeral were left to me.
That day in February changed my life,
Overnight I grew up - became a man at 29.
Little did I know, more was yet to come.
Life is hard, life is grim,
But if thrown in you must learn to swim.

I have survived the holocaust,
The cost to me was horrendous.
I will and never can be the same.
It will be with me until the day I die.

Carl Kemper

For Michael

Forty years ago
Our separate lives
Were joined
A delicate thread
Invisible as a spider's web
Bound us as one
Yet left us free
To be ourselves.
Through the years
That thread grew stronger
But never shackled us.
It would stretch
To infinite lengths
Just holding us gently
With a loving touch.
So here we are
Still individual
Yet a pair
Still bound together
Yet free
To be us.
Thank you for all those years.

Shirley Roberts

The Gift Of Music

A musician is an artist
Painting a picture with sound;
The melody builds up slowly -
Note by note the theme is found;
Each one builds up to make chords
To fill spaces in each phrase;
The timing then decided
Doing something to amaze -
To keep the listener's ear attuned
To a new, uncommon blend
Of double notes and trebles
With the basses to attend
And playing altogether
A new song is inspired,
Fast or slow, soft or loud,
A new air to be admired.

So again the pattern begins to form
And the melody makes itself known;
Soon the writing and playing are merging
And another 'invention' is born.

There is no end to the wonder
Of the musical beauty of sound
When the soul is inspired to search
Till the notes of the song are all found.

Joan Moore

Thoughts On A Burns Night

What would Robert Burns have thought
If he could see us now?
Would he condone this feast of meats
Whilst still the homeless roam the streets
Or would he inwardly recite
Payne's homilies on human rights?

I wonder, would he see his past
As history has portrayed
Would he enjoy the adulation
They partying and celebration
Or would he have a further plane
To gear the energies of Man?

What would Robbie Burns have thought
Or women's liberation?
Would he approve of absent mothers
Or women mangers as lovers
Or would he think, as some do now,
That women may have too much power?

Could he accept the speed of life,
Or would he seek retreat?
Could he write about our times,
In rhythmic verse and flowing lines,
Or would he find the pace too fast
And yearn for times that now are past?

Much has been written of Robbie Burns
His life, his times, his style,
But none can look into his soul
And therefore cannot know the whole
This still remains a mystery
To be discussed by such as we.

Sylvia Betts

Angels Near

I feel my angels near
I try to tell them my fears
They are around us every day
Guarding, guiding, helping us on our way
You just need to ask them
As they cannot intervene
Unless asked
Tell them your earthly problems
And they will try to please
To smooth your way and
Bring good things, both this and
Every other day
Remember to say thank you
Never think it's not enough
They will stay beside you
Helping to guide you
Something may occur
It's your angels' way of being there for you
Always remember they are there and
They really do care.

Linda Ann Marriott

Crich Stand

High on a hill in Derbyshire it stands for all to see.
It has so many memories that mean a lot to me.
It is an inland lighthouse, 100 feet above the sea,
In memory of Sherwood Foresters
who gave their lives for you and me.
You can see it standing high from many miles away,
It light shines out as darkness falls at the end of every day.
And every weary traveller is guided on his way.

Patricia Lee

Husband Material

Looking for a husband can be a long chase
But you have to have patience if you want to win the race

Harry was a charmer; he took me to a dance
There he met a buxom blonde, I knew I'd missed my chance

Then I met John, oh what a lovely man
I told him that I liked him and away he ran

Now Dennis was amusing, in fact really funny
He spoilt it all the day he asked me for some money

David was great, we had a great life
Until the day I found he already had a wife

But undeterred and not downcast I thought I'd try again
I met Paul, so clever and handsome and so very, very vain

But I believe that somewhere, there's a man for me
He may not be rich and handsome, but he'll be kind you see

I once read a fairy story and really ever since
I know you have to kiss a lot of frogs
Before you meet your prince!

Jan Wilson

Swallows

As I sit here on a summer's eve
Watching the swallows as they speed
They come to see me every day
Twittering and chattering all the way
Soon they will go home, to a land far away
And I know they will be back
Next year, some day.

Eileen Robinson

Baby

A baby -Stanley,
a tiny body not allowed to live,
but he lives in our hearts,
we made room for him,

we remember him;
because we needed him.
He sleeps now:
a credence to our need.

Alone is he - yet not.
We shall have him one day
with a soul
when all flesh shall see.

He will be prepared for us:
greet us,
show us;
because he was there, before we were.

Kathleen Bartholomew

Scenes Of Night

The harvest moon with her golden glow,
Shedding her light on the country below,
Stars that glitter like precious jewels,
A hooting owl intent on prey,
Seeking food before start of day.

Bats that dart between the trees,
Catching moths on the evening breeze.

Before my eyes the stars that shimmer
Suddenly start to become much dimmer.
The moon, she glides slowly away,
At last it is the start of day.

Josephine Riley

Reverie

I saw there today, belovéd
As dreams invaded sleep
On soaring wings reflected
In oceans' bluest deep

I heard thee today, belovéd
Which caused my heart to leap
Leviathan beside me
As if a watch I keep
I felt thee today, belovéd
Your arm so close to mine
Like breath of infant sleeping
So soft and so divine

I sought thee today, belovéd
In cavern dark and wide
My heart forever beating
Beating with the tide

I've lost thee o belovéd
And only I can know
The thoughts that haunt me even
Of love so long ago.

Maureen Barnett

Harry Patch

It's ninety years since the war
A proud man sat, poppy near his heart
Far wiser than the rest.
'Don't forget the Germans,' he said
a tear in his eye,
It made me cry.

So brave and true
His love shone through
They gave their lives
For me and you!
God bless them.

Ann Humphrey

Fear

Blood pounds through my ears
as the panic flows through my body
my heart thuds in my chest
and sweat breaks out on my skin
my hands begin to shake
and my body trembles as it gets closer and closer
thoughts race through my mind
as to what it could be
I turn as I hear a sound
my mind screaming
blood freezing in my veins
your eyes so cold, unfeeling
the end is coming near
I can see it in your cold, dead eyes
I can feel it in the air around me
I open my mouth to scream
but no sound escapes
then it's over
the end.

Sandra Minnikin

Shine A Light

Shine a light on me, so bright for all to see,
One that shines through until eternity.
So strong a light that never goes out,
Making questions, but never doubt.
Giving sense of strength that shines through.
Light, oh light, what can I do
To make you shine on me?
Darkness will die as stillness and calm arrive,
Like bees around a honey hive.
Bright light of love, with no shadows around,
Making me dizzy, going round and round.
I can wait, light so bright, for that cheer
Of joy, I want to enhance.
My smile widens from ear to ear,
Shine that light and give a chance,
Bring out the best that got lost,
Giving it all, at no cost,
Oh bright light, so bright
Shine on me.

Jacqui Page

My Pop Star Friend

(To my friend, Sir Cliff)

'Do you believe in destiny?'
a pop star once said to me
as he held me tight
on an autumn night
for all the world to see.

Sadly he had to go away
so we never got together
but I'm so proud
when I hear out loud
the song he wrote for me.

I'll never forget
my pop star friend
and the way things used to be
we were young when we met
and he's famous
and yet -
he stills sings that song
for me . . .

Marie Haswell

The Border Sign Croeso Cymru

(Welcome to Wales)

No Croeso Cymru needed I,
for when the border came
the grasses started singing
and the hills all called my name.

The hedges whispered, 'Welcome'
As the miles hurried by
And everything was smiling
In the land that met my eye.

There was no need for music
When all nature played the tune
And harped upon my heartstrings
From the sunrise till the moon.

When I heard the lilting voices
Felt the soft rain's sweet caress,
No Croeso Cymru needed I –
What more could it express?

Elizabeth Morris

For Stewart And Mary

A daughter born to Stewart and Mary,
The months have been long
And the days have been many,
And now, from the darkness and into the light
This angel appears, Thank God, she's alright.

Little pink fingers and little pink toes,
Lovely blue eyes and little snub nose,
The answer to all your hopes and dreams,
Nothing else matters, or so it seems.

But caring for this little mite,
Even if you get no sleep at night,
You've waited so long for this bundle of joy,
Now you'll be buying a cuddly toy.

The pair of you will be so happy,
Even if it's always 'Change that nappy.'
In the years ahead you'll see her grow,
Her love for you she'll always show.

A happy family you've become,
Now you're a proud dad and she's a happy mum,
May she be lucky and have good health
A nice personality, and maybe some wealth.

And as she treads along life's way
You'll never forget this special day.
God's gift to you was long overdue,
Congratulations and best wishes
To all three of you!

Edith Mee

End Of An Era

I'm standing alone in the hallway,
The telephone's on the floor.
The first time the house has been empty
Since nineteen seventy four.

The removal men have long since gone
And I must be going too.
But there's time to go up to the lounge
For one last look at the view.

I stand at the big picture window
And gaze south west to the sea,
Just as I've done for thirty-three years;
Oh well . . . what will be will be.

I shift my gaze to the garden seat,
Where Ruth and I sipped our wine,
On warm summer evenings, watching bats
And hearing the church bells chime.

The old male blackbird catches my eye,
Fluttering down to the seat;
Outside the window, cocking his head
Looking for currants to eat.

My son is waiting out in the road,
I finally check the keys,
Then slam the front door and feel on my face
A gentle south west sea breeze.

Number thirty-five Hawthorn Park Road
Has gone as we round the bend.
I blink back the tears and swallow hard,
An era has come to an end.

Rex Duncan

Peace At Last

(In memory of Harry Patch)

Another tomb in the graveyard,
the last of many now laid to rest,
memories remain forever with him,
old age, has decried his final resting place.

Many years of reminiscing
His thoughts - those of his alone,
Many of which, had he been given the chance
He'd have chosen never to own.

A fighter - for his country,
Loyal to Crown and King,
With little choice but to go forth
With others who were never to return
Paying the ultimate price that war brings.

A hero - so he was told,
Medals, 'worn deservedly on his chest,
Peace at last -
For one who lived to tell the tale
Who now returns to join those he'd once known,
Who by war, only with death
Were ever blessed.

Bakewell Burt

The Humble Bee

The humble bee
Does quite a lot for you and me
Pollinates the shrubs
And flower and blossom
On the trees.

The bee has a lonely life
But he's quite unique
Think of his busy time
Flying back and forth
Carrying all that nectar
To his hive.

Leave the flowers in your gardens
So the bees can do their job
And we can see the beauty
And colours with our eyes.

If it wasn't for the bees
No fruit and veg
No honey with your bread
And the earth would go barren
And everything would die.

Be thankful for food on the table
Winter time bees are nowhere to be found.

Janet Hannan

Wishing And Hoping

I have an ache in my heart
That never goes away,
It is with me always
Through every night and day.

I find distractions of every kind
To put this worry out of my mind.
But though I try - hard as I can
There's a name haunts me - Afghanistan.

At times I've broken down and cried,
To hear yet another brave soldier has died.
I think, oh no, please not another,
My thoughts turn to their wife or mother.

Oh how I long and pray for the day
When on the TV news they will say -
The war is ended in Afghanistan
We will bring all our troops home - soon as we can!

What a day of rejoicing that will be
We will all rush outside and yell *'Yippee!'*

E Catherine Gray

Seasons

And so sweet Nature's force is spent
Her sap retreating through the trees
Soon old Winter's grip will freeze
And rent his anger to bring her to her knees
The beauty of her mantle is shed
It takes its leave and bids adios
Rustling underfoot, disappearing from our view
She is only sleeping for as while
Gaining strength to rise anew
To free herself from Nature's guile
What force is this? As Spring comes into view
What lies behind this yearly enterprise?
With seasons as they turn and blend
With regularity each year
They apprehend each other's time as they reappear
As the season come and go
We keep them in our minds
Each with its special beauty show
And memories they leave behind
Each has its special flavour
We keep within our hearts
To look forward to and savour
As each year departs.

John Hewing

On The Edge Of A Dream

Fleeting glimpses flashing on the inner eye,
something, someone alluring, running away,
always tantalisingly just out of perception,
peeping around corners, looking back.

Colours, elastic rainbows stretch away into one brilliant light
against which shadows flicker madly,
like a magic lantern show out of control.

Soundless music begging to be heard,
notes in graphic caricature dance hand in hand
down a long shaft of sunlight
or is it a moonbeam?

The tenuous hold on never never land slips away,
unrealised the illusion fades,
running through the sieve of memory.
I know it was fabulous, sans artist, sans composer
sans wizard,
I can only imagine the magic.

Richard Hackney

The Visit

It was her godmother's
That weary brown suitcase
Packed neatly into
Her allotted visit
And met so dutifully
On platform four.
Their journey home polite
In time for lunch
No wine but only water
Thins out their talk
Of ordinary and every day -
What time to take her nap
How much to give
On the collection plate
And though the room
Accommodates
Her modest taste
The laminate cannot
Replace a carpet.

Julia White

Human Destiny

Searching, seeking signs of life
Europa scanned and dunes of Mars
We are never ever satisfied
We've trod the moon, we'll reach the stars

We'll walk under suns of blue and red
On water worlds with monsters dread
On planets of ice and burning sand
We'll meet strange life in stranger land

A lifetime from our sun and Earth
Light years from our place of birth
We'll mutate, evolve, move on
Till what makes us human will be gone

Nomads without roots put down
Home, no planet, nor city, nor town
We'll journey on from star to star
Ranging the galaxy wide and far

A fantasy? That, you might say
But where would we all be today
Without those with a fantastic dream
Querying realities for what they seem?

R L Cooper

Let The Privet Flower

Let the privet flower for the bumblebee
Don't clip it into formality
Let the birds sing
Let the frogs croak
Don't stifle Nature as she grows
Don't prune the hedge
So there is no dog rose
Don't in winter flail the berries from the hedge
They feed the birds when there is little else
Don't play with the fish within the stream
Let Nature be! enjoy her as she is
Savour the wind and the lightning flash
Relish the snow and the kiss of the rain
Listen to the birds as they trill and sing
Admire the buzzard as he circles the air, a king
Do as little as possible to cause harm
To all God's creatures of every type
Don't believe Man's media hype
Be only gentle to all and sundry
Sail your boat only by the wind
Always remember, be Nature's friend.

Paul Gamble

Through A Child's Eyes

Quietly manipulating silence.
A child with eyes aglow.
Wanting so little, yet
Needing so much.
Silently manoeuvring
The quiet sadness of her life.

One day, like any other,
Becoming so unlike,
In the intensity of the moment.
Something out of nothing
Anything being a nonentity,
In the sadness of her life.

The child's eyes, wet with tears unshed.
Reflecting her sorrow
In thoughts of tomorrow.
Undecided in an unnatural world,
Screamings of the Earth,
In a long-forgotten life.

Noise only taking over
When minds are full.
Loneliness in a crowded room.
Vibration of the music
Thumping with the beat.
The beat of her heart.

Hearts and flowers, her love unleashed,
Flames of anger, hot coals, her eyes
Burning into her soul.
Once, long ago
The love of an older brother,
Uppermost in the realms of reality.

Dreams became nightmares
The suddenness of death through a child's eyes,
Became a burden.
Childish behaviour and adult immaturity
Locked the chains and
Put a padlock on her life.

As the weeks became years
Now a teenager, still a child,
Breakdown.
Nerves shot full of tranquillisers.
Hospitalisation.
Her only future,
A child, transformed into a monster.

Fighting, struggling
With her inner demons.
Afraid to live, even more afraid to die.
Mis-used, abused.
Running for safety,
Away from pain.

Grief, coming to terms with death,
Never getting the chance to say goodbye.
Flowers, reams of flowers
But nowhere to lay them.
As the ashes are blown,
Blown to the four winds.

At the summit of her mountain
And the valley of her tears.
A wave goodbye.
The coolness of the wind
And the suddenness of rain.
Earth and skies converge,
A shout, 'Goodbye.'

Pamela Green

Five Hundred Metres Above The City

Five hundred metres above the city
I, tracing the wintry silhouettes of the trees opposite
See revealed in Nature's time
Those hazy outlines pushing through
A cloak of green.
Spring anew.
And looking around it warms me so,
The daffs in bloom
The cowslips and iris too
There! Early tulips in a row.
And now, I know that spring
Has reached me from below.

Deana Constable

I Can't Believe It's True

To see one's poems in print, is such an uplifting thing.
Knowing it will be read and real joy it will bring.
I never thought for one moment they would publish mine
That was until I discovered Forward Press and then I did find
My poems were to be published
I could not believe my eyes
I read the letter of acceptance with eyes that were open wide.
I will be forever grateful for the opportunity for my work to be read,
I can not get over it, I can't get it out of my head.
Because I am just a simple man who seems to dream a lot,
But at last, thanks to Forward Press, satisfaction I have got.
To know my poems will still be read when I am dead and gone,
This fills my heart with happiness I often burst into song.
Why should such a simple man have so much success?
One thing I will admit, is I always tried my best.

Don Goodwin

My Comeuppance

I went to do some 'keep fit' at the local school,
In footless tights and leotard
I really felt quite cool.
I left my dangly earrings on
I thought they looked quite fetching,
Until I nearly blacked my eye
When we had to do some stretching.
Then, my beads, they had to go,
The heavy bits were pinging
Into the young mum next to me
As our bodies we were swinging.
Now she didn't need to shout like that,
I didn't mean to bruise her
And oh! That simply was not true!
How could I confuse her?
Well, I had my hour of glory
When we had to touch our toes
But I shouldn't have kept my belt on
It cut off where my blood flows . . .
Now they were very sympathetic
And they showed that they did care,
When they sat me in a corner . . .
With my feet up in the air!
Now someone might have warned me
About how the times have changed,
I'd appeared from the back of a time warp,
Inn my seventies glamour range.
These young mums were quite casual,
Very minimal with gear,
It was unbejewelled tracksuits
And an iPod in one ear.
I just wanted to blend in discreetly
Like years ago when no one would scoff,
At a younger and more petite me
. . . who was secretly showing off!

Patricia Anne Withnall

The Lord Of The Vineyard

In the Lord's great vineyard
There grew a special vine
From which the Lord had promised
Would flow the sweetest wine.

Watered by the gentle rain
Pruned with love and care,
Blessed by days of soft, warm sun,
Full, perfect fruit it bear.

Those branches which refused to yield
The Lord cut from the vine,
Others he cleansed carefully,
The grapes grew smooth and fine.

Yet this Lord was troubled for
Other vines which were lost.
He knew a way to save them
But he also knew the cost.

For the goodness of that vine
To reach each withering life,
The vine must be surrendered
To the gatherer's knife.

As the vine's life slipped away
The other vines shone bright
And filled the Lord's great vineyard
With the precious vine's own light.

Yet where the vine once flourished
The Lord's tears fell like rain
They washed and cleansed and purified
So the vine could live again.

Then the Lord rejoiced to see his land
So perfect and complete.
Each vine fed by that precious vine
Producing wine so sweet.

To those who stay grafted to that vine
Abundant life He'll give.
The vine will fill and yet sustain
So drink the Lord's wine and live.

Jean Cullop

A Reflection Of Perfection

Oh for the perception of Your vigilant eyes
That I might recognise righteousness and right through disguise
Oh that I could listen with Your attentive ear
So the cries of the silent man's heart I could hear
To speak with Your tongue, if only I could
I'd speak words of wisdom and never falsehood
Oh for the span of Your welcoming hands
To reach out to people across all the lands
Oh for the strength of Your ever willing shoulders
To carry the burdens of tired Christian soldiers
Oh to reflect Your most sacred heart of gold
To show love for millions of people untold
To be ever faithful, humble and pure
To give love like Yours Lord, that's for ever sure.

Marlene Doy

Crete

A magical wedding and honeymoon in Crete
Agios Nikolaos was where we stayed
A picturesque harbour behind which mountains meet
Lovely memories which never fade

An exquisite white dress with bow, sequins and lace
Excited, happy and in love
We pose for our photos together, face to face
God watches down on us from up above

The sun shines down into a sparkling sea
With sky so clear and blue
With my handsome husband right beside me
From today our life starts anew

In the wedding limousine I feel like a queen
The Greek people smile and wave
In my beautiful dress I feel so serene
All these precious moments I shall save.

Lisa Pease

The Overlooked Investment

Why do we invest so much time
In our work and daily chores
And spend so little time with our children?
Their lives we tend to ignore

Why do we exhaust ourselves
Rising early and going to bed late
Eating the bread of anxious toil
Busy making our mark on this world we populate?

Overlooking the one investment, our children
Who matter more than anything else, thus
Solomon said, 'Children are a heritage from the Lord'
An invaluable legacy He has bequeathed us

'Like arrows in the hand of a warrior'
So are the children of one's youth, yours and mine
Is his striking smile
Nothing is more worthy of our energy and time

There is no need to work all day and night
Time for our children must be met
Trust in the Lord, He will provide
Our lasting legacy, an investment we'll never regret.

Catherine M Armstrong

Unpronounceable

That's what you are.

Via email and chat rooms
I've come to know you
As £$-er)-21

Liar emails and chat rooms
I've come to show you
My £$-er)-21

Spyware emails and chat rooms
I've come to s and m
On m s n

To yabadaba-yahoo

chatroom
that room
where there's
no know-
ing things
for sure.

A lie supplies a cheap thrill
and meaningful relationships are just a mouse click away.

press <enter> to con me.

Andy Jenkinson

My Birthday Wish For You

My birthday wish for you
Is happiness, forever new
I hope it lasts your whole life through
As will my love, so very true.

My kiss was so sincerely meant
I know my love is Heaven sent
You must have been made for me
So let our friendship always be.

My gift to you, to keep you warm
From wind and rain and heavy storm
I never want to know alarm
To know you're always safe from harm.

I miss you so when you have gone
When you have left me all alone
My thoughts are for you all the time
Please tell me soon, when you'll be mine.

I want to tell you through this rhyme
The way I've loved you many times
Our kisses all so tenderly
Ever meant from you to me.

Until my heart forgets to beat
You'll be my love when e'er we meet
When will you let your feelings come
Then only will you know I've won.

John Pierrepont

A Walk Through Pines

I walk softly through the sunlit scented pinewood
Crisp brown needles crackle underfoot
The scent of sandalwood fills the air
It brings me happiness to be here.

The air is alive with the sound of splitting pine cones
Seeds fly in the wind
Nature's confetti in my hair.

Two roe deer up ahead,
Stop me dead in my tracks
They stare back at me awhile
Then their tails aloft, white flags fly
And wave goodbye.

My little dog is beside me,
We know these paths by heart
A long-eared owl blinks his distaste
As sunlight filters through and shines upon his face.
He spreads his wings and flies.

A fox ambles across the track
Very confident, he doesn't look back
Squirrels cry out in surprise
We continue on our way
My dog and I keep up a good pace
How we love this secret green, inviting place.

Once more I deeply breathe in its earthy scent
Before we bid reluctant farewell
Homeward bound.

N J Brocks

My Agoraphobia

In 1983 you came back into my life,
Bringing me nothing but trouble and strife.
You kept me a prisoner in my own home,
When all I longed for was to go out alone.
You caused me pain, you made me cry,
I felt so ill, I thought I would die.
From doctor to doctor from pillar to post,
Where o where is the cure I wanted most?
Where exactly does the answer lie?
Eventually I found it in a doctor called Di.
She gave me the will to carry on and fight,
I fought so hard with all of my might.
The shops in the village seemed so very far away,
If only I could go out, just for one single day.
I tried and tried, the tears, the pain,
It was a battle, lose or gain,.
I gave it everything, yes everything I had,
It wasn't easy, in fact it was very bad.
In 1990 after 7 long years.
A lot of heartache, many tears,
I was starting to win the battle of getting out of the door,
With each day I was doing more and more.
But there were still so many things I couldn't do alone,
Still so many jobs that had to be done on the phone.
I could now walk to the shops, there and back,
Get the groceries, take them home and unpack.
But still I couldn't get a bus into town on my own,
Only if I had someone to go with, borrowed on loan.
It took several more years of heartbreak and pain,
Before I could finally travel alone again.
May 2nd 2000, I jumped on a bus and popped into town,
It was just like my world had turned upside down.
Here I was, free at last
Finally free to forget the past.
So I decided to do something I had never done before,
I started college, part time,
each day I couldn't wait to get out the door.
To catch my bus, to feel like I had finally rejoined the human race,
Living life at a hectic pace.
Going to college at age 53,

Really did do wonders for me.
The computer course was harder that I thought it would be,
But others in the class helped me.
Our tutor, June, was really nice,
Always ready with her advice.
Now I really feel I have turned my life completely around,
With this new freedom I have found.
With a lot of help from my husband and son
The battle is now over, finally won.
So it's goodbye agoraphobia, you belong to the past,
Never again will you get me in your grasp.

Pat Dring

Broken

She sighed a breath of hurt and pain,
Forlorn and helpless there she lay
Her sobs so deep and harrowing,
For her love and loyalty she'll pay.

The empty wound inside her heart,
The dull ache left behind.
Longing for the one she will never have,
So why the torture in her mind?

How can this be? For why? She asks,
Punished, chastised and condemned.
Her mind, her heart, her shattered soul,
Her hopes and dreams come to an end.

She softly cries herself to sleep,
She dreams of reaching for his hand.
But how can this be? For why? She asks
And yet she will never really understand.

She will close her eyes and be at peace,
For whilst she sleeps she feels no pain.
Safe in the place of happy dreams,
Until the morning comes again.

Sharon Reed

A Christmas Wish

It's that time of year again, as snow falls
Where are you now?
For here I am alone this year
Since the day you walked out
A reflection in the window
But it's not you I know
A ghost of Christmas past appears,
When love seemed made for us.

Christmas Eve, a sound in the hall,
It's the clock sounding for midnight.
I hear the sound of a church choir
And dream of our last time.
Candles around a log fire
As we shared our favourite wine
To love we raised a glass, to our future
And hoped it would last a lifetime.

Church bells are ringing out aloud,
It's Christmas day I know,
All around are celebrating
But my heart's empty and cold.
I need to have you back forever
And never let you go.
A ghost of Christmas future
Without your love to share
I'll walk alone in the drifting snow
And look to a new year without you.
Everybody's celebrating Christmas time,
But I'm hurting inside.
Everybody's celebrating Christmas time.
I wish you were here tonight.

Roy PJ Mullin

Nature Red

Predators and prey,
each have their part to play,
reliant on each other.

Take the lithe jaguar,
creature of sheer terror,
sheathed in beauty.

Or take his prey,
heart bursting deer,
elegant in fear.

Both waiting, bated breath,
for life or bloody death,
unbearably aware
of one another.

Stan Solomons

Stroll In The Outwoods

Coruscating light on blades of grass lush with dew.
Cascades of blue,
faint, shadowed in dappled sunlight,
creep sinuously through tangled undergrowth,
over rough ground
carpeting twisted roots.
An overlay of sapphire hue
amongst gnarled trees
majestically striving towards the sky,
filtering daylight on soft bark paths amid shale and soil.
A gentle breeze, coolly, caressingly
whispers through ancient pines.
We stroll, your hand in mine.
This is our moment.
Our own special time.

Julia Richdale Ellis

A Better World

In ages past, in darker times
A light shone through to guide us.
A way of life, to save our souls,
With love and song in chorus.

We see the world and wonder why
Power and greed divert us.
Is Nature's hand, alone, enough
To bind us all in purpose?

We come and go and leave our mark,
We choose a path to follow.
Let's strive to leave a better world
For those who come tomorrow.

Colin Hinds

Misplaced Time

Misplaced time
unspent days
- thinking of ways
to rewrite the past

Splitting my mind
half a smile
- it's been a while
since I was present

Opening eyes
closing doors
- life held in pause
a future in sight.

Sadie Brown

The Spider And The Fly

The millionaire lay sick on his bed
his mind an infernal blank,
except for some thoughts of stocks and shares
and fortune lodged with a Swiss bank.
Thank God he'd no need to fear being ill
though he did feel a trifle depressed,
still he'd summoned the
cream of the medical world
and his wealth would take care of the rest.

The consultant came wearing a 'toothpaste' smile,
combined with a manner imperious
and then proceeded with terrible guile
to pretend he could find nothing serious;
but the millionaire was used to false smiles
and no longer had faith in a fellow
who could not explain why his nose had turned blue
and the whites of his eyes bright yellow.

Whilst the sick man lay wondering what to do next
his gaze settled onto a spider,
weaving her very own web of deceit
with only her instincts to guide her;
when a gullible fly came ambling along
becoming ensnared in her thread,
the spider adopted a 'toothpaste' smile
until the poor fly was dead.

The rich man then knew that the medical man
was treating him just like that fly,
with his insane grin he was taking him in
and waiting for him to die.
He suddenly knew what he had to do
to show his brain power undiminished,
he sprang out of bed and tightened a cord
until the consultant was finished.

Said the millionaire when they took him away,
repeatedly asking him, 'Why?'
'To show that old fool that *I was the spider*
and not as he thought, *the fly.*'

Jessie Smith

A Joy To Behold

The countryside in spring
Is a joy to behold
A sea of golden gorse
Before your eyes unfold
Buttercups in meadows
With painted heads of gold
Horse chestnut blooms
Like candles big and bold
Whispering grasses
Standing proud and tall
Misty blue wisteria
Cascading down a wall
Willow trees bowing
In a soft and gentle breeze
Bright yellow clusters
Draped on laburnum trees
A carpet of bluebells
In a shaded wood
Rhododendrons bringing forth
Many a bud
Wild lupins growing
On a pebbled shore
Red roses climbing
Around a cottage door
Hawthorne hedges
All smothered in white
The countryside in spring
A breathtaking sight.

Brenda M Hadley

Out Of Body Experience

A very strange thing happened
To me, the other day.
I came right out of my body
In a very funny way.

I was floating up behind it
And I could not get back in,
I was drifting like a shadow
And was feeling very thin.

How this thing had happened
I could not really say.
My mind was in a turmoil,
This was really a bad day!

My whole being was pulsating
And completely out of breath.
If I did not catch my body
I knew this could be my death.

My body turned a corner
And it went right out of sight.
Then I began to panic,
I was in both shock and fright.

I kept on chasing after it,
Then it began to rain,
I skidded through my body
And came back together again!

Denise Angood

Memories

Memories are treasures, locked in the heart,
With thoughts of days that are gone,
They stay with us forever,
As the years go on and on.

We think of our childhood and teenage years
And those far off, carefree days,
Life was very different then,
In oh so many ways.

Photographs bring such memories,
Some make us sad I know,
But we smile at all the fashions
Of the days so long ago.

Wonderful holidays we don't forget
And so many Christmases gone,
Weddings and parties, laughter and tears
And the memory lingers on.

Some of our memories are secrets,
Thoughts that will always remain,
We think of all those days gone by
As we wander down Memory Lane.

We often remember those who are gone
And wish that they could be here,
But we only have a memory,
A precious souvenir.

Good times and bad times, all in the past,
Some things we do regret,
Too late, too late, how sad those words,
But we do not forget.

We dream of all those far off times
And the many joys that we knew,
We have such wonderful memories,
To cheer us whatever we do.

Christina Burnell

Decidedly Deciduous

When I was younger I was oh so sure
That I was an evergreen.
Through every season, for evermore
I would retain a springtime sheen.
I thought of me as an evergreen tree
With a bloom I would retain.
The sheen of spring would stay with me
Why should it not remain?
Through summer's span it would continue
Blessed with a perennial energy.
In autumn too, still have springtime hue
Seasons would not bother me.
But latterly, maturity brings a reality
The leaves are tinged with gold.
They reveal to me with clarity
The signs of my growing old.
Soon I will be less green
My ageing limbs you and all will see.
That green springtime sheen
Diminished in autumn's maturity.
Now I am older I am sure
It is clearly obvious.
That sheen of green is no more
I am most decidedly deciduous.

Stan Coombs

Why

Why are we afraid to say no
When the world is crying out for love?
Why do we avoid smiling or a cheery word
We just frown and pass by
Enveloped in gossip
About the negative world?
Why not smile as we pass by
Lighten people's day
Instead of saying, 'Why, why, why?'

Melvin Dean

Anonymous

I keep on the move, travelling from town to town, city to city.
Sometimes I hitch or catch a bus,
If finances permit I'll catch a train.
I'm not going anywhere really,
Arriving wherever I end up,
Staying a few days.
I had it all,
A wife, a home, successful job,
Until it all went, on that fateful day.
I sleep in bedsits, sometimes doorways,
On the beach, or empty houses.
A few days work in cafes or bars,
Pays for some food and a drink to escape.
Making friends is all in the past,
On my own, I keep my wits and stay safe.
I keep running to escape my past,
The sadness, the happiness,
A life that's gone.
My life is now different,
I'll always be on the move,
To forget,
I will always be anonymous.

Colin Griffiths

My Hall Of Residence

In my heart Normanby Hall still belongs to the Sheffield family.
It is situated on a surrounding estate full of trees waving happily.
To the visitors who come to see a pageantry of historical flowers,
That nestle under the majestic and magnificent umbrella-like towers.

Near a village, three miles from the town of Scunthorpe
And covering the approach are walls of dry-stone, coloured taupe.
Then as you enter on the main parkland estate
With Isis governing the blue peacock's springtime fate.

And all the mallard ducks and Canadian ducks and geese,
Bringing joy to the children and the parents a sense of peace.
There is also horse riding and events
for the more adventurous person.
And summer rallies including that of steam engines
for your immersion.

Then in autumn, when the bucks go through their seasonal rutting,
Ready for the next doe's annual spring debutante gathering.
Allowing these ladies to set a future romantic date,
At 'My Hall of Residence' to seal a beautiful matrimonial fate.

Anthony Newton

What A Wonderful Life

Children walking, skipping, playing down the street they go.
The uniform of days past. Wellies, T-shirts and shorts, torn.
Leg bruises and grass cuts and black fingernails that form
Trophies of summer holidays, so proudly and bravely born.

Boggy land with high reeds as tall as towers for cover
Make for wonderful dens and places for hide and seek.
The hang and drop tree, a magical sense of danger.
Cowboys and Indians, Robin Hood and the Lone Ranger.

A life of carefree play with only our imaginations to use.
Children of fifty years past had everything needed.
So healthy and yes, dirty, but so full of freedom and joys,
With the whole council estate, girls and boys.

Skipping in the street, cops and robbers, rounders too,
No matter where the ball lands, in which of the gardens,
Always a child from one of the houses down the street.
A multitude of laughter, happiness and endless running feet.

Mothers sometimes joined in and took the skipping rope,
Hot sunny days and warm balmy evenings to play games.
No school tomorrow, allowed to stay up longer at night.
Pure bliss of games played, what a wonderful sight.

If a picture be taken of those halcyon days once lived,
With the scruffy, grubby children, with wide happy smiles,
Having nothing compared to what children have to day,
Only the best of childhood in every single, possible way.

Sheila Ellen Wright

Noon

It's twelve o'clock.
I am waiting for the patter of children's feet,
As they come into my tuck shop,
At the corner of the street.

Sarah Jane loves lollipops,
With red and yellow stripes,
Young Freddie wants the liquorice
That looks like Grandpa's pipes.

Jamie chooses chocolate mice,
Peter he goes for sherbet,
'Can I have two gobstoppers,
To take home for brother Herbert?'

Jelly babies for Freda,
Tommy's a Milky Way,
'Hurry up,' says Charlie,
'Or we shan't have time for play.'

Paul decided on bubblegum,
Sam a Lucky Dip,
Lucy was the one to
Choose a raspberry flip.

Their tuck bags clutched very tight,
They go off on their way,
Such happy smiling faces
It always makes my day.

Pauline Vinters

Show Me

Show me
The river
That runs
Nice and clean
Show me
Where I can
Dip my feet
Show me
The place
I can sit
And look
At life
In general
Show me
The mountains
Where I can
Wonder·
And think
Show me
The place
I can
Sit in peace
Show me
The wonders
That are all around
You have
To be in
The right place
Each time
Show me
The man
That will
Look me
In the eye
Say hello
Instead of
Looking down
Show me
The friend
That will

Always be there
Show me
The person
That will
Never let
Me down
Oh, yes
It's myself
For crying
Out loud
Show me
Love's strong
When I am
With you
My eyes
Have seen enough
My heart
Has too . . .

Sharon Lambley

The Daisy

What view is this that greets my peaceful sky?
Fair mistress outward peeks on grassy mound.
What dress of white encapsulates thine eye -
The yellow sun with dancing maidens round?
This angel innocence had played its part;
A pleasing flow'r that now outshines them all
And found a fool to give away the heart.
Deceiver, queen of dung, you stand, you fall,
A question lingers soft on fettered lips -
To plant the thought in mind and soul decreed.
How strange to think of such amusing quips -
A simple flower, complicated weed?
On dais stands what Nature thus creates,
In soft, majestic beauty contemplates.

Jenny Amery

The Last Of The Many

It has been said,
Some believe it true,
Old soldiers never die
Or so it seemed,
For two old men.
But, yes, they do.
The parting and the journey
To that distant land
Of Pan's lost boys.
Extraordinary ordinaries.
One saw the grey leviathans
Exchanging blows at
Jutland's naval match;
Harry Allingham aged 112,
The other Harry Patch at 109,
Last man at Paschendaele
Exchanging quarrels with the foe.
Now they are gone,
Joining so many lads
Eclipsed in youth
By busy guns.
Flying over the rainbow
Of women's tears.
Gone, but not forgotten.
A history book is shut.
The Great War they called it then,
The last war,
There would be no conflict.
How wrong they were.
A never-ending story.
Written by mankind;
Man made in the image
Of his brutal god.
Perhaps.
It does not matter.
Our humble heroes
Have laid their poppies,
Their final remembering,
Remembering.
Now we must remember them
Shaped on the last of war.
Not the First of the Few
But the Last of the Many.

Peter Godfrey

I Close My Eyes Yet I Can See

I close my eyes and listen.
It's a wild thought
And a grand thought
And a thought that comes from within.
If ever there was a thought to think
I think this would be the thing.
I've seen the measure
Of dreams on my mind
I've heard the sounds of a song
And silent thoughts
Are part of the time

And I know where they belong.
From sounds of sea
And scenes of skies
And cavernous caves
And eagle's cries
Mellowed and muted
Like the leaves on a tree.
And thoughts are part
Of the thoughts I see.
And a wild thought
On the brink of my mind
That I can portray
Though my eyes are blind.

For my mind is free
As free as the wind
That wildly sways
The trees and me.
I can feel the wind
The wild, wild wind
And that's enough
To make me see.

A wild thought
And a wild, wild breeze
Wilder and wilder as I bring
My thoughts to bear
On the sounds that are there.
With the smell of the breeze
And the wind in my hair
I close my eyes
And I can see.

Joan Elizabeth Blissett

Locked In The Church
Or The Old Carpet Sweeper

(a true story)

'It was only an old carpet sweeper
But still it could pick up the dust,
It was only an old carpet sweeper
But now it lies mangled and bust.'

One day, at the ladies' meeting,
Proceedings were peaceful and calm;
There was no sign of what would soon happen,
No sign of that fearful alarm!

One by one the dear ladies departed,
Till just Rosie was left in the church;
In the Ladies' she rinsed her hands quickly,
Unaware she was left in the lurch!

'Twas a moment of doom when the pianist
Pushed the door to go into the hall;
Not an inch would it budge, for 'twas bolted,
Leaving Rosie to desp'rately call.

In fact Rosie shouted and hollered
And knocked, cried out, rattled and screamed;
'Twas no use, there was no one to hear her,
Nor anyone coming that e'en!

Then - a moment of increasing horror,
Realising now what must be done,
For the glass in door must be broken,
To let out the poor, hapless one!

What to use was the next sombre question,
Soon answered by a stroke of luck,
An old carpet sweeper was spotted,
A sturdy old eater of muck!

'Twas the work of a moment to take it,
To swing it so hard at the glass
And several hard swings made it break it,
Till voilá! Here's freedom at last!

There remained only one major hurdle,
How now to get out and go home,

For the gates at the front were all padlocked
And the pianist had no mobile phone.
A kind girl came right near to Rosie
And heard her distraught pleas for help,
So she gave her phone to phone Pastor,
Who came to assist her himself.

It will make Rosie cautious forever,
When in church she prepares to go home,
So when you go where she went, remember -
Be safe and take sweeper and phone!

'It was only an old carpet sweeper
But still it could pick up the dust,
It was only an old carpet sweeper
But now it lies mangled - and bust.'

Rosemary Eades

My Thanks To . . .

I'd like to thank the chip-shop,
For the aroma that is heaven,
I could eat fish and chips any day,
Once, twice, or six or seven.

I'd like to thank the ice cream van,
It's the music I love to hear,
I could eat an ice cream, anytime of year.

I'd like to thank the fairground,
For the excitement and all the fun,
I could eat candyfloss and a toffee apple,
Then have another one.

I'd like to thank the doctor,
Who caused such a riot,
Said I'd been overeating
And put me on a diet!

Stephanie Lynn Teasdale

A Church Is . . .

Silence folding and unfolding
A stone tape holding prayers and psalms, loud with praise
In echoes of moments from long-ago days
Coloured glass that dances, swings, turns to dazzle stone aisles
Tears, exhortations, anguish and joy
Solemn adult faces and children's smiles
Vows and devotion, those promises made to keep
Marble monuments beneath which past patrons sleep
A golden cockerel's glittering promise beneath a rainbow's arc
The beacon of jewel-bright windows, comforting after dark
Joy at life's beginning and sadness at the ending of its days
Dust motes sprinkling with gold the evening air
Dog-eared books of prayer and parables well told
Voices that rise and swell, competing with the bells' pealing
Squashy, fat footstools with embroidery worn pale
By constant kneeling
Wood, smoothed by work roughened hands
Funeral wreaths, smoky candles and wedding bands
Families, generations
Prayers, pleas and venerations
Echoes of hatred, blood, sweat, toil
Praise to the Lord for the fruits of the soil
Stone walls
A nave, aisle, steeple
But above all else
A church is *people.*

Sheila Sharpe

About Candy

Candy, the likes of you, there was no other,
At six weeks old you came from your mother,
Till fourteen you did live,
That's what the good Lord did give.
You were so young and free,
Fetching the biggest boulders from the sea,
Running in the park
And wanting to stay till it was dark.

Then for Bobby, the kitten, you did care,
Washing his ears till they were nearly bare,
You were gentle with everyone you knew
And you were a good guard dog too.

These are the memories we have left,
That's why we feel a little bereft,
But now you are free from pain,
So our loss is your gain.
Seems like yesterday your life had just begun,
Now we say thanks for the laughter, sorrow and the fun.
Sleep tight sweet Candy Kiss,
You're the one we'll all miss.

Sandra Elliker

Pacific

Manta rays
Soar upon wings
Of black, brown, cream and white
Caressing currents to nurture their flight
Clams
In spawning exhalation
Freely flow into
Clouded currents of creation

This is their home
These oceans of turbulent turquoise
These forests of gleaming emerald
These corals of garnet glow
This surf of scintillating sapphire
Where breakers of diamond brightness
Splinter the sand of amber fire
And rocks of opal moonshine
Reflect fish eyes of opulent ruby
And sea urchin spikes of gold refined
Where all that glitters is
Pacific mined.

Cecelia Cran

Limbo

Dancing on a cloud of freedom
Dancing with eternal joy
Where the earthly voice of passion
Cannot e'er that sound destroy
Looking backwards to the future
Looking forward to the past
Rhythmic time now lost in wonder
Where life's pendulum halts at last
Many decades stand in limbo
Centuries or only weeks
Who can see the past or future?
No one knows and no one seeks
Dancing on a cloud of mystery
Drifting through eternal void
Gone all pain now lost in history
Wrapped in peace and overjoyed
Rhythmic time is caught in wonder
Where and when is journey's end?
But this is not ours to ponder
We will go where He will send.

Juliet C Eaton

I Will Lead The Way

As I lay on the battlefield
Killed by a sniper's bullet in my head
God came to me and said, 'Arise My son,
I'm going to make you a leading angel,
Large white wings and a crown on your head.
Bring Me up to Heaven all the blind and wounded
I will restore their sight and heal their wounds.
I can perform miracles,
That's why this place is called Heaven.'
'May I ask one more miracle?
Stop nations fighting each other,
Let us all live in peace and harmony
Instead of turning the world into a place of despair,
Otherwise my death will have been in vain.'

Gordon Dangerfield

Framework Knitters

Dead, wooden bobbins
Faded coloured wool on cones
Stand now in case alone
Yet still revive
The all pervasive stench of oil
Still reflect grey complexions
Dim eyes creased into the knitter's frowns
In ill-lit room

Ratchets come down
Poverty knocks, still echoing
The dull throb of loom
Feet move again in rhythmic
Melancholy dirge
Singing the knitters' song
Of life barely lived upon the bobbin's verge.

Jessica Heafield

Solitude

Water rippling over stone,
Down the walls, where moss had grown,
Under the bridge, the stream still flows,
On and on and on it goes.

On the bank wild flowers grow,
Branches of willow tree hang low,
Stirring in the gentle breeze,
Touching the water's edge with ease.

Buttercup, primrose, cowslip gold,
Showing their colours, bright and bold,
Pebbles beneath the water shine,
Ivy and columbine entwine.

Birds swoop down to water's edge,
Leaving their nests high in the hedge,
They look for insects to feed their young,
To many waterside plants they've clung.

Daisies, open to face the sun,
Will close again when day is done,
So much quiet life around,
Stay for hours without a sound.

Except the rippling of the stream,
Which lulls you into a hazy dream,
Losing all account of time,
All adds up to the sublime.

So this must be solitude,
In future over which to brood
And as each summer comes around,
To these thoughts we will be bound.

Elizabeth Stockley

Christian Thoughts

If I can make a life a little brighter
By kindly word or deed or friendly smile
Or perhaps to make a load a little lighter
By walking with a friend that extra mile
If I can turn a soul away from sorrow
To comfort them amid their grief and pain,
And know the sun will shine again tomorrow
For sunshine always follows after rain.

If I can do my duty to another
Just one good deed for each and every day
Perhaps to help a sister or brother
To walk in peace and faith on God's highway
If I can keep my little candle burning
To show the way to wanderers in distress
And make a pathway brighter at each turning
Bringing to each life some happiness.

If I can help when all around seems dreary
When everything in life is upside down
If I can keep on smiling and be cheery
And speak a kindly word that ends a frown
If I can aim to be just like my Maker
Giving to each day my very best
If I can be a giver not a taker
Then I may feel that I am truly blessed.

Tom Hanson

Pictures From The Mind

The pictures he draws in your mind,
Are not those of the hanging kind.

His pictures will not hang in a frame,
They are gently placed inside your brain.

The written words, some down in rhyme,
For you to read, retreat in time.

I speak of those whose words go far,
Down to Earth or touch a star.

Of people, places, love and pain,
Or children playing in the rain.

Teardrops, feelings, butterflies,
Stern, strong men with pleading cries.

He loves his work, may act a fool,
He loves to write, the pen his tool.

The poet of whom I speak,
To match his thoughts, great words he'll seek.

His feelings, thoughts, lay deep within,
When poem ended, again begin.

Creative mind, forever flowing,
Inventing pictures for your showing.

Roy Taylor

Pets

Tiny creatures - big eyes -
Ears on side of head.
Trusting you as they leave their mummies
Established at home
Growing and sometime ruling the roost.
Having babies of their own,
Making you an honorary grandparent.
Fully grown and still living in that special place
In your heart
Old now - maybe deaf -
Eyesight not too good
Venerable beings
In your world and home.
Fateful day -
Called to romp and play as tiny creatures -
Big eyes - ears on side of head
Once more in your imagination and heart.

Goodbye all my faithful pets
I truly loved you all.

Jane Day

Father And Mother

Oh Father Sun
And Mother Earth
You mean so much to me
Have you been around
For all eternity?

A golden disc
So way up high
Your light it travels fast
May you be forever there
Always shall you last.

The Earth it is our mother
A living, breathing being
Dancing round in circles
Spinning, feeling, seeing.

We think we are the masters
Of this globe of inner fire
Never really thinking
Of what she might desire.

Errol Kavan

Night-Time

Night-time has crept up on me again
Like a fever that gets under your skin
And my shadow is a lonely soul
Drifting aimlessly into escapism

Night-time has a blanket of stars
Reaching far beyond their existence
Astral travelling in syncopation
Heading towards a cosmic explosion

Night-time has slept with me again
And my conscience is playing with my mind
Like a beautiful dream, put on hold
Whispering its caress in my ear
Night-time is pouring its troubles
Into the abyss.

Teresa Billington

My Son

If I could turn the clock back
To the year of '34,
To see into the future
And got to know, what's more.

I think I would have changed things,
But not so for my son,
As he is my one and only,
So that's a task well done!

He has been a good one
And of him I'm very proud,
From the house I really miss him,
But not so in a crowd!

I pick him out above the rest
And thank God that he was sent,
For, my son, I really love you!
And you are the very best!

Janet Brown

Beginnings

(For Vera)

For now you find yourself at a new beginning
You've found yourself at a brand new start,
from the pain that you've felt inside
Loved ones will carry you to their hearts.
From the storm clouds of winter
Comes the freshness of a new year's spring,
As our prayers drift on the morning breeze, this is your time
To start believing again.

Like the force of the largest waves
Your strength will come shining through,
You could part the deepest oceans
And turn the greyest sky to blue.
You could jump higher than the comets
And shine through the brightest stars,
You could heal those who suffer
By showing the world who you really are.

Just like the passion of a rose
Like the corals in our sea,
Your strength will conquer mountains
Your love lasting for eternity.
With the guidance of an angel
Your heart will become another's dream,
With your hearts joined together
Destiny will treat you like a queen.

With the sorrow that you've felt
This shall all be left behind,
With the warmth from the sun
A new love will be by your side.
To give their life for you
To walk that extra mile,
Showing you it can be a beautiful world
Just to see your glowing smile.

So this your time now
By deciding which path to take,
Remembering whichever path you choose
Just take things day by day.

Richard Michael Grew

You Told Me I Was A Great Dancer . . .

You loved the way I moved.
I met you at a Spalding disco
Though I'd seen you many times before.
I took you home in my old blue Skoda;
Your dad had a massive record collection
(like a library it was)
you showed it to me
while he was upstairs alone,
in bed, sleeping, snoring, innocent.
You'd been going out with the Slow Tea drummer,
he told me you were a cool chick,
(today they would call you a 'babe'.
Your dad, the one upstairs, sleeping, snoring, innocent)
Had played with Pink Floyd
On their album 'Atom Heart Mother'
He was a music lecturer at a local tech.
I was mixing with rock royalty.
But he was alone upstairs,
sleeping, snoring, in bed, innocent,
still, his vibes were downstairs.

You did a lot of swimming
every day at the council pool,
many lengths of breaststroke,
I gazed in admiration,
I said, 'Let's make love on the sofa,'
and finally, after a little bit of arguing,
you agreed.
(Your dad, still upstairs, sleeping, snoring, innocent,
dreaming of the next Pink Floyd album).
We made passionate love on that sofa.
I felt your skin, the soft, fleshy arms
of a perpetual swimmer,
the faint, sexy smell of chlorine,
you made a lot of noise
I kept wanting to ask you
about the Floyd and 'Atom Heart Mother,'
but I resolved to concentrate
on the present job in hand.

After a few minutes, you agreed to a second date.
Yes, you were very keen - no problem there.

The following night, 7.30 in fact.
Savouring the prospect all day long
I turned up well on time
in my old blue Skoda;
your dad answered the door;
he was small, bald, boring,
wore tiny, professorial glasses, highly
conservative clothes, even a thin grey tie,
pin stripe shirt, shoes,
'Hush Puppies' were they?
he didn't call me 'man'
in fact he didn't know me.
I said, 'I've come to pick up Lucy,
we've got a date tonight.'
He said, 'I'm sorry, she's gone out.'
And, without further ceremony
closed the heavy door.
I never saw you again.
(but at least I met your dad)
the one who played tuba
in the orchestra
on 'Atom Heart Mother'
if you listen carefully you can hear him.
He must have been
the one in the third row,
second from the left.
Any chance of an autograph?
It's never too late.
By the way, Lucy,
what actually happened
with regard to that promised
second date?

Tyrone Dalby

He's Coming Home

Mist hovered way across the field and in the early morning
light with air, still chilled,
I stood an gazed along the lane to where the branch did meet
the road,
And watched intently at the spot where vehicle movement
could be seen
And there, as every moment passed I craved
he'd soon be in my sight
And then, with lengthening beam of light, the lane before me
was now filled.

My arms across me now held tight my shoulder wrap
and quickening, my heart did race
As through the swirl of morning haze the light
engulfed the space between.
With movement pressed upon the stones as wheels did turn and beams were sent
towards the west,
Then, all before me now was dimmed and very soon
each moving part did rest.

Behind the mist the glow of sun with fingers spreading ever wide
And soon, the gentle touch of hands does cause my heart
to quicken pace
Then, strong arms are holding tight and love's deepest surge explodes inside
For now, at last, we are as one, as passionately I kiss his face.

Rosie Oakes

Cancer - The Curse Of Life Today

(Loss of a family member and friend to cancer inspired me to pen these lines)

The stainless steel structure is rigid, bright and strong,
Gleaming in the morning light, its life seems surely long,
But can this simple picture be a mere false façade?
Could it not just crumple, like a flimsy piece of card?

The length of its existence is uncertain at this stage,
And learns to take the knocks that shock, from every living page,
But time is of the essence, when the blows they leave no marks,
And a bomb, it waits so anxiously, for those vital sparks.

Then one day it happens, and its ugly face does rise
And cause the steel structure to gasp with great surprise,
The vital spark has flickered and the time is passing fast,
This rigid, gleaming structure now knows it may not last.

Within this rigid framework, there is a living curse,
That spreads throughout the structure,
getting worse, and worse, and worse,
Degenerative evil, takes o'er the structure that was bright,
And whisks away a vital life, in the darkest hour of night.

There is no obvious answer, to this curse that rules the Earth,
Any structure, plant or being, may just carry it from birth,
We hope the day will come soon, when the curse will lose its hold,
And the brilliance of the medical world a cure will then unfold.

Then the stainless steel structure, that is rigid, bright and strong,
Will constantly be gleaming, in a life that's surely long.

Nigel Lloyd Maltby

That Fateful Day

We go through life fearing death
We wait on that day with bated breath
When that fateful day arrives
The day we dread all our lives

So what has life been about?
Full of heartache, full of doubt
With a little love thrown in now and again
A little love to ease the pain

But the pain comes back, fear never goes away
The fear of that frightful pending day
We know not how and we know not why
We know not when we are doomed to die

But die we will, that's for sure
So they tell us! That's God's law
Who are they to know it all?
The day will come when they will fall

So go through life, don't let it get you down
Wipe away that worried frown
Wear a smile each and every day
Until that day you pass away.

J Hillas

Untitled

Hey diddle diddle
MPs on the fiddle
The speaker crashed out in a swoon
The media laughed to see such fun
And the greedy will go - none too soon.

David Peniston-Bird

Farewell To My Son

(Memories of my son, who died in the aftermath of 9/11 in Manhattan, New York)

You took us to the airport, on the last day of our stay.
We spent a lovely fortnight with you and Holly in the USA
It was the holiday of a lifetime and you were the perfect guide,
To all the special places in which you took such pride.
'This is my backyard now Mum, I want you to see me in it
and picture me when you get home, whenever you've a minute.'
We took so many photographs to remind us where we'd been
And build a store of memories of all that we had seen.
And as you stood and waved to us as we got onto the plane,
We never dreamed it was the last time we would ever see you again.
You live on in my memory; and maybe time will ease the pain,
Of losing you, so suddenly and I'm sure we'll meet again.
When there will be no barriers between our time and space
And I will come and find you and once more see your face.
And now, when day is ending and the evening has begun,
I sit and think about you, I'm so proud you are my son.

Gwendoline Bennett

Memories

I sit in the dark, my mind running wild,
Remembering the things from when I was a child,
Like speak when you're spoken to and don't stare about
And just talk quietly, no need to shout.
Don't forget to say thank you or send a note,
You can say so much in the few words you wrote
These things, when a child, you hated to hear,
But one of these days as the years go by,
Those words will come forward, forget you needn't try,
But then it is so nice when children you don't know,
Will hold a door and wait for you to go,
You will thank your parents looking down from above,
All the things they taught you were sent with love.

Diane Young

'With Thee Is The Fountain Of Life: In Thy Light Shall We See Light'

(Psalm 36.9)

Jesus, Thou source of all true good,
Fountain of life and light and love,
All that the Father has is Thine,
Brought down to earth from heaven above.

In Thee is life, the life of God,
To raise our souls from death and sin;
O do Thy quickening work in men,
O put Thy living power within.

In Thee is light, the light of God,
To make men see their darkened mind;
O draw men to Thy holy word,
O open eyes that now are blind.

In Thee is love, the love of God,
To pardon, bless, heal and restore;
O come with that pure love to men,
O make us seek Thee more and more.

True fountain of all gifts from God,
All wisdom, truth and power and grace,
Come and enrich our poor, frail lives
Until we see Thee face to face.

Margaret Siddans

Significant Others

Let me count the ways I love thee
Poets of the female gender
Moments that bid me a precious good morning
Imagery I long remember.
Through secret windings of the afternoon
I pluck a handful of posies at will
They who know the true scent of a rose
And aerial wings that thrill
I skip at the feet - treading perfume
Of those who spread cowslips pretty
O world there are so many who do the trick
Poetesses abound like windblown confetti.
With sweet-scented rhythm
They punch a hole in the blue
Waving or drowning at rainbow's ending
The drops on our cheeks are not tears but dew.

So if in time I emerge in deep purple
With a cheeky red hat worn askew
Proudly displaying that which I'm savouring
With other hopeful poets I'll join the queue.
Scheming schemes of how to win over my hero
With cocoa and carroty stew
Or dreaming dreams contemplating the onion
Moonstruck as a Valentine addressing you
Carol Ann Duffy, worthy winner of the Poet Laureate prize
The first moonshining lady to run rings around the guys.

Lucy Green

Meditation On My Christmas Cards

As I study my collection of cards
Kings on camels, shepherds and stars -
I wonder, *did it happen?*
Or is it a legend that lasted two thousand years?
But then - even mythology needs some foundation -
A start - a seed - a root
From which to sprout.
Something certainly happened around the sleeping sheep
To make those shepherds tremble - then shout -
You can explain it away by saying
That folks were simple in those days
And a comet - could it be? a dramatic sight at night
But why mention a message of comfort and joy in that context?
Is that invention?
It makes no sense!
A man was born
He lived and died
Of that there is proof
As for the rest -
Even the oddest stories often
Turn out to be the truth.

Maggie Camps

Gifts

Firelight in the evening
Comfort in a chair
Knowing someone loves you
Smiling, just being there
Music drifting slowly
Feeling safe and warm
It's little things that matter
Give shelter from the storm.

Sunshine in a garden
Deckchair placed in shade
Sounds of someone mowing
In a distant glade
Somewhere children laughing
Playing by a stream
It's little things that matter
When you've time to dream.

You could not buy these feelings
They have no price you see
A world full of treasure
Is given to us quite free.

Pauline Hill

Sleepy Head

Wake up, wake up, you sleepy head
A new day is dawning
Put on your woollies
Get out your sledge
And greet the snow this morning
Wake up and hear the robin sing
Listen to the church bells ring
There's porridge cooking in the pot
Snowballs to make, such a lot
Come on, come on, get out of bed
Our snowman yet has no head
Sliding we'll go, down the hill
Doesn't matter if we have a spill
When we're cold and we tire
Chestnuts are ready near the fire
There's stew in the oven too
Will be ready to warm us through
So get up, get up, you sleepy head
Let's have you up and out of bed.

Eileen Henderson

Despair

How can I explain how I feel, is it my age?
Older in years but much younger in mind,
Eager to turn to the next page.
To me the years have been most kind,
I am so wrapped in love,
I must have been out of my mind to despair.
But still it is there, this feeling of despair.
Why do I dwell on the news?
Keeping my own old fashioned views.
I would like to change the world,
No cruelty, no wars, a world full of love.
So here we are, back to square one,
Maybe my despair has gone!
Maybe, we should finish with a song!

Jean Dutfield

The Dance Of Nature
A Spring Romance Of Butterflies And Bees

Oh, how the butterflies flutter by;
So briefly, like the people you meet in life,
Briefly, they stop, smile at you;
To say hello and then:
They are gone, with no time left to say goodbye.
As bees fly away from the flowers;
As every man is born each day,
As every woman cries for a nostalgic trip,
Oh, how we try;
To build a bridge for love,
Nobody sees the real truth;
And now it's gone.
Stop! Make a wish!
Oh, for goodness;
Let's dance and take chances again.

Richard Chapman

The Raging Terror

The raging terror in the tormented mind
For dark clouds prevail
And as the tears of a clown are never far behind
And as the terror lurks in the dark shadows
Of the tormented mind.
The dark voices whisper their dark, deadly thoughts
Of kill or hurt a total stranger
And still the dark clouds prevail
In the dark shadows of
The sad, tormented mind.

Michael Spittles

Searching The Summer Breeze

Searching the summer breeze
for council, my eyes
tramping across the clouds.

Several birds come to eye me
and the trees sound like the sea,
gently moving in time to the corn.
Many movements in the azure sky
clouds enquire for the weather.
Black stroppy horizons gathering.
Then stabbing rain
into lightning strikes.
Down from the darkness
now everywhere on
sky and land.

Doreen Sylvester

The House Knew

The front door slammed of its own accord,
It no longer waited for the prompting shove of my hand,
It knew the score!
It had been there before.

The settee, once evenly balanced,
Now groaned at the uneven one-sided weight.

The cooker ran screaming!
It hid behind its old ally, the fridge
And yelled, 'No, not toast again!'
The fridge, being empty . . .
Kept its thoughts to itself.

It would appear
The house knew love had gone
So . . .
Why don't I?

Stephen Green

I Spied A Bonny Lass

On a moonless night I spied a bonny lass,
Where the stars shine brightest,
My love was lovelier like a ghost,
A phantom that brought me suffering.

And my spirit died discovering,
Her beautiful incandescent light,
While meditating I saw Madame
Holding alighted candelabra,

With the rush of the wind and sea,
Came a phantom on the lee,
Hysterical, we belong together
My lovely lady and me.

That I spied a bonny lass,
The art of painting pictures with words,
Like a cabbage butterfly,
Excited by the perfume of lavender.

Intoxicated by delicate smells of the garden,
As Madame walks, taking in all the pleasures,
Of Nature's glorious landscapes,
Whilst reading and reciting love poetry.

So cheerful, gay and bright,
O'er yonder by the foaming sea,
As happiest as can be,
Like the beautiful face of a climbing clematis.

Stunning, complimenting grace and charm,
Courting my sweetheart, I love loyalty,
While succumbing to the fancies of love
In the age of the romantics.

Kindness like a diamond-studded crown,
The old rectory where our love began,
Unequivocally blessed with beautiful memories,
With your standard flag flying in the mist.

I spied a bonny lass while composing muse,
That I kissed her eyes and face so passionately,
O my sweetest darling underneath summer blossoms.
How beautiful and romantic can it be.

James Stephen Cameron

Shuttered

What was wanted,
for a must surely be
A roundabout inside,
no one knows the spoken,
only what's to see.

You came out of where?
Gave nothing to be held.
So long it's been wanted,
so long, I don't remember,
an eternal restless ember.

For what was once promised,
I pass on will never be.
For time has laid its lines,
has turned it all around,
has left me only times.

So I will never realise a dream.
unable to live with guilt,
too kind to be a level,
too controlled to scream,
too shaded to be full.

I'll live half a person.
smile to all who dislike.
Swallow the pain in shadow.
Keep a mind half able
and add another fable.

Paula Johnson

An Ode For Forward Press

Congratulations on reaching your 21st year
Forward Press do really care
Help poets young and old
Nobody left out in the cold

All different themes
Helping poets' dreams
Even story tellers
Some get best sellers

Forward Press helps us start
They really do have heart
Publishing poems, stories as well
Which they even sell

Forward Press give me inspiration
For me to write a creation
They help me progress
Which could lead to success

Forward Press I would like to say
I wish to thank you if I may
Hope some day my poems will pay
Forward press have a really good day.

Pat Hunter

Leaving Home

Today I lost my only son
He left home to have some fun
He is only twenty-one
That's why I'm feeling rather glum.

I gritted my teeth and said goodbye
Determined that I would not cry
I turned my back but with a sigh
I won't miss him - it's a lie.

He left home on Sunday night
Will he cope and be alright?
Will his hair soon look a sight?
I have lost my shining light.

I will remember him all my days
If he copes I'll be amazed
Because of how he's been raised
How I'll miss his funny ways.

But hark, is that the telephone?
Is it him phoning home?
Is he feeling all alone?
'Mum, I'm broke,' I hear him moan.

'How I miss your Sunday roast
I am living on burnt toast
Please put money in the post'
At last - 'Mum I love you most.'

Isobel Cosford

Statutes Fair

The village, veiled beneath an early haze,
awake already for the Statutes fair.
Smocks, skirts and aprons starched and ironed white,
baskets overflowing, children contrite.

Awake all ready for the Statutes fair,
families flock to the decked market place,
baskets overflowing and the children contrite.
A jumbled patchwork patterns the mown grass.

Families flock to the decked market place
there's a stilt walker juggling, music plays,
a jumbled patchwork patterns the mown grass
and round a high cart, barefoot boys cluster.

There's a stilt walker juggling, music plays.
Men trade names as sounds melt the parting haze
and round a high cart, barefoot boys cluster
with buxom, flat-faced, pole-thin, whey-faced girls.

Men trades names as sounds melt the parting haze,
George, Jenny, Alfie, May, 'See you next year?'
from buxom, flat-faced, pole-thin, whey-faced girls,
'Hire me, let me tell you about myself.'

George, Jenny, Alfie, May, 'See you next year?'
Smell the pies, puddings, peas, earth, sweat and fear.
'Hire me, let me tell you about myself,
please. I need to work for another year.'

Smell the pies, puddings, peas, earth, sweat and fear,
of workless days, cold nights, no bed or food.
'Please, I need to work for another year,
shilling a day to feed my growing brood.'

Maddy Scott

Sestina

Raging the covers back I check my watch
Again another dream thrown out of order.
Woken up to fumble a cigarette
And taste the only nearest thing to happy
Anymore, the smoke begins to act
Like magic, if you know it feels that way.

Some nights, when those are longest anyway,
You lie there crying, mad and burning, watch
The slow unwind, feel yourself react
Remembering against the doctor's order
Let her go, your own fearful life happy,
Curled under the covers with your cigarette.

The girl who found you for a cigarette
Whose name you weren't too sure and like the way
She holds it, careless, for a moment happy.
The midnight TV room turned low to watch
Her ruffle down, T-shirt all disorder
Without the staff remind her how to act.

Another mask behind a circus act
She hides elusive, one more cigarette.
Her vocals hushed before the final order
No one hears and won't reveal the way
She lumps there deep in secret and you watch
Mistaking how her face is lit so happy.

When the dying shine, relaxed and happy,
Kissing goodnight and bow their final act,
You never know with them and only watch
Her go, leaving the taste of cigarette
Unfinished in your mouth, you drift away
In thoughts refusing you to sort in order.

Given a decent friend, a different order
Of disaster, maybe even turned out happy,
The night unravelling itself her way
Where she was falling, caught her in the act
As old and empty as the cigarette
That smoulders into ash and while you watch

You lose the order, trying to enact
A happy ending, as the cigarette
Burns away like seconds from your watch.

Gregory Whitehead

One Of The Wind

The way you speak is strange my friend
For truly thou can't see the wind,
Yet still you say it with sincerity
Describing it and its severity
Yes, I see, the trees that blow
But cannot see the strong wind though.

I see dark clouds that stream on by,
The ire in the turbulent sky
I see these things I have no doubt
Umbrellas each blown inside out
I see the rain that Nature sends
But cannot see the wind my friend.

I see huge hailstones pound the ground
Like children's stonties I'll be bound
I see them roll and roll around
Then simply vanish to astound
Yet hard as might and might as may
I cannot see the wind thou say.

I see the birds in desperate plight
To keep control during their flight
I see these things upon this day
But cannot see the wind thou say.

I see strange poems blowing by
Juggling like a butterfly
I see tall grass, how it waves
The high flown kite and how it braves
Yet though I try, I fail to see
The wind thou say, thou can, to me.

I see the destruction everywhere
Rooftops lifting here and there
I see lean chimneys tumbling down
In crumpled heaps upon the ground.

I see the oceans lash the shore
Rising sixty feet or more
I see sweet flowers, how they bend
But I cannot see the wind, my friend.

Peter Terence Ridgway

We Are One

We are one,
Without inhaling
We cannot exhale.
We are one.

The words we speak breathe out our beliefs,
Our morals,
Our moods,
To be inhaled by the world.
We are one.

The actions we take breathe out our love,
Our hopes,
Our efforts,
To be inhaled by the world.
We are one.

The thoughts we have breathe out our compassion,
Our resilience,
Our respect,
To be inhaled by the world.
We are one.

One is a symbol of unity,
It is the symbol of community.
It signifies the universe,
It signifies the single effect of a single person.
You are not one,
We are one;
One breath,
One world,
One hope.

Claire Walsh

Let's Pretend

(Dedicated to Clare Elizabeth and Amy Victoria)

Let's pretend that
your favourite cuddly toy can speak.
As your best friend he's with you all the time.
If he could speak he would say, 'I love you and you are my friend.'
He's very grubby, a bit tatty, but oh so cuddled.
The one and only toy and no other is quite the same.
Is he a teddy, or is she a doll?
Perhaps a cuddly elephant, or maybe a rabbit.
He goes everywhere with you. The park, the shops, on trips.
And cuddles you in bed.
He's your very best friend when you're tired or poorly.
If he could speak, he'd say, 'Cuddle me, hug me.'
When he's very old and you're grown up,
Will you still love your favourite cuddles?
What is the name of your best loved toy?
Then . . .
Let's pretend that
School was just for one day a week!
Yes, on a Friday. The very best day of the week.
Lunch packed, swim gear and gym kit and all your favourite games,
So much to do in one day.
A special and magical day that was extra long,
with lots of play times and fun and the sun was shining all Friday long
Just imagine, the teachers would give you extra marks
and never get cross,
and no one fell out and everybody won at games.
Then the children changed places with the teachers!
So much to do and such a lovely day.
For Friday's are special and so exciting.
Which game do you choose?
It's such fun pretending!

Elizabeth Hayden-Jones

Venus

Soft brown pools, rich dark hair
the goddess drives men to despair
visions of Roma instilled this fight,
this chariot, that breaks men's will.

They call her name, but no voice is heard
as darkness muffles broken word
A soft hand reaches into their open chest
as hearts are filled with her caress

She is Venus, she causes so much pain
lovers love, sets hearts to flame
But once the love is gone, subdued,
broken wills, a multitude.

Reach down inside and feel this love
that warns the soul from gods above
For Venus has so many names
true love the savage wolf it tames.

Paul Williams

The Rise And Fall Of Love

You broke my heart in record time
And acted like there was no such crime
I dragged myself from the mud
And now damn, I'm looking good

The limelight now shines on me
So that everyone can see
How much of a fool I was
To believe that you were God

You showered me with flowers and praise
Which seemed like forever, but was barely days
These gifts however were untrue
For someone else was loving you

You are my only life forever
And we will never be together.

Natasha Watkins

She Is Milady Gaia

She is judged a great beauty.
A female of infinite charm,
Who sails into one's presence
Like the fabled Queen of Sheba.
She does not crave attention,
Yet she is a hit every season,
She is as regal as good Queen Bess,
Despite rising from humble beginnings,
Like the fairy tale put-upon Cinderella.
One of the dwellers on Mount Olympus.
Folk say she is wise beyond years,
Who show kindness and understanding.
She is as learned as Madam Marie Curie.
Equal to any male who challenges her.
At times she flaunts her power and status,
As changes are needed for us to progress.
She's as fragrant as heady scented roses
Or the summer heat on a summer meadow.
As graceful as a gliding white swan,
On a full moonlit pool at midnight.
Ready to converse on any subject,
The subject of every male's desire.
Inspires painters and poets to be creative.
To complete visionary images and sonnets.
Where she walks spring pretty flowers,
A retinue of butterflies dance about her.
Busy bees declare her to be their queen,
She, after all, is the immortal Lady Gaia.
The great spirit of our burgeoning planet.
The divine vessel who carries Man's seed.

John Pegg

Missing This Enclave's Master

How can I explain how much I miss him?
His presence in the house and garden,
Or attending to the beehives and queens,
I told them immediately he passed over.
It's a duty allocated to his successor,
Otherwise the colonies sicken and die.
The old cat, Smoky, lies upon my lap,
He lies there purring a lamentation.
Strange how our domestic animals
Seem aware of the death in the family.
He who was attuned to this landscape,
His roots were deeply wedded
To this beguiling enclave about me.
Carved out of the great shire forest,
By his forbears forty generations ago.
They arrived before the Norman conquest,
A melding of Celts, Angles and Saxons.
Felled the giant trees to form the fields,
His family roots are deeply embedded,
As the oaks, by the axe, they conquered.
I go to his den in the old garden shed,
Where he hid from my daunting Mother,
As if his absence would be noticed.
His briar pipe he'd stuff with Condor,
Bubbling demijohns of elderflower wine,
Neglected, are badly in need of racking.
His portable radio and sagging deckchair,
Garden catalogues and used seed packets
I feel his wraith remains contented.
Here he muses, planning the year ahead.

Julia Pegg

Dear Anji . . .

(Geoffrey 06/05/46 - 20/11/06)

A single red rose sits on your table,
I'd buy you another if I were able,

I long to tell you how I'm still near,
your woes my dear, I always hear,

I wish, I wish, I could touch your face,
stroke your hair, share a loving embrace,

tell you how much I love you still,
it never stops, it never will,

I think you know this, you know me true,
no one could love me as you do,

the bond we had does not break,
even though your heart does ache,

I sit beside, guard your sleep,
long to wipe the tears you weep,

sometimes you feel me, know I'm there,
stood behind you smelling your hair,

I wish I could whisper into your ear,
I've not left my love, I'm stood right here,

I'm going nowhere, I'll be always with you,
deep in your heart you know this too,

there was no one else for me in my life
just you, my friend, my soul mate, my wife.

Clare Milsom

And In The Morning We Will Remember Them

(Ex R M P)

Left, right, left, right
Down the ramp we go
Left, right, left, right
Steady lads, steady!
Hold him tight
Left, right, left, right
This lad we carry
Did he know Harry?
Left, right, left, right
Covered with a Union Flag
Home he comes
Left, right, left, right
Home, he has arrived
A family full of grief
Left, right, left, right
A family proud
With the time he had served
Left, right, left, right
'The Last Post'
Is heard for this soldier
Coming home from
Afghanistan.

Frank Baggaley

In Memory Of My Soulmate

(Written in memory of my late husband Michael, who passed away on 24 Dec 2007 after a long battle with cancer)

Your memory is deep in my heart;
Remembering the happy times we shared together.
Michael, Michael, where are you?
Michael you are at rest,
You kept me on my toes
And swept away my woes.

Sue Herschell

Who Can Paint A Butterfly?

Who can paint a butterfly?
No one else but thee,
As they flit from flower to flower,
On our buddleia tree,
I think of the Creator,
Who worked a work of art,
Their patterns are so exquisite,
That they lift the fainting heart.

These gorgeous little creatures
Are a wonder to behold,
And in fact, they tell a story
Which is waiting to be told.
That we too can rise from dormancy
And rise to heights above,
With the help of our dear Maker
And the Saviour's love.

Sheila Richardson

Woodland Dreams

Dusty, stony pathways and rippling streams
Sweet-scented wild honeysuckle
Sun bursting through the trees
The smell of the earth after the rain

A vivid mass of blue flashes before my eyes
And the scent of bluebells fills my heart with joy.

Birds sing upon the branches
A deer stares through the trees.
One could almost imagine fairies and pixies
Playing here among the trees.

Jean Bailey

Nonsense

No sense of time, no sense of taste, no sense of wondering,
no sense of waste.
No sense of humour, no sense of love, no sense of touch,
fits like a glove
No sense of balance, no sense of speed, no sense of caring,
no hope, just greed.

No sense of harmony, no sense of sight, no sense of fear,
can't see the light.

No sense of hearing, no sense of smell, no sense worrying,
nowhere to dwell.
No sense of knowing, no sense of thought, no sense of feeling,
no wonder distraught.
No sense of hatred, no sense of sound, no sense of loving
as bombs hit the ground.
No sense of tenderness, no sense of passion, no sense of forgiveness, seems it's
the fashion.
No sense of shame, no sense of doubt,
I'm beginning to wonder what these words are about.

B Baxter

Step-Parenthood

Two little faces that carried a tear
Are now those faces that I hold dear

Two little hearts, I thought wouldn't be mine
Are now so precious, so true, divine

Two pairs of eyes that I thought I wouldn't see
How much I wanted this family

Two little heads, so bright, so tough
I thought I'd never be good enough

Two little souls, bear with each mistake
As their step-mum is learning each step to take

I cannot thank you enough - so much was at stake
I'll love you forever, my Sophie and Jake.

Lisa Quinn

Scary Hair Day

Nana loved Bat, but Bat just love to tease,
So on Hallowe'en when she was queen,
Bat just had a scream.
'Ha-ha,' screamed Bat, 'That skirt's too big.'
but Nana didn't care, the only thing she cared about was doing up her hair.

'You look a fright!' called Bat to her from around the kitchen table.
But Nana took his cheeky words as a compliment with flavour.
So was all dressed up like a scary old witch,
But her hair was rollered up, the rollers were still heating.

'I do look nice, I'll scare a few, sand Nana full of glee.
But Bat was full of laughter and fell off the settee.
'You'll never scare anyone,' he cheekily admitted.
But Nana didn't care, she thought she looked pretty.

'A witch I am and never wrong,' she replied to Mr Cheeky,
but Cheeky Bat still had to grin as her rollers were now steaming.
Then with a poof and a bang, Nana ran off screaming.
She looked into the mirror seeing her hair green and gleaming.
A frizzy mop of hair with a green grass tint.
Bat flapped along to see with a great big grin.

'This is fun,' he sniggered in a stuttering remark,
'I said you looked silly from the very start.'

Nana turned to face him, steam puffing from her ears, crying,
'I really wanted to be the beautiful queen of witches!
You did this on purpose, you saw me going green!'

But now in trouble, Bat flapped away and hid,
He had to do something, he had to think quick.
Flapping into the air Bat started to sing.
'She was no pretty picture and many she did scare,
and do you know the funniest thing, she had a frizzy mop of hair.'

'So I am the queen of the witches and I'll scare them all.'
And Bat turned and laughed because there was no queen at all.
But Nana didn't care, she was having fun.
She turned and ran towards him.
'Flap Bat . . . here I come.
Grr!'

Cas Lake

Careers Advice

I have fallen out with Death.
It was not a great loss,
we were more acquaintances than friends,
I just got sick of him, complaining all the time.
Not a day went by without him complaining about his job
and what he had to do,
but it was his own choice.

When he was younger he could have done anything,
but he just wanted an easy life,
to appear more threatening than he was,
he just wanted to dress in black, wear white make-up
and listen to The Cure.

Mr Green, the careers advisor,
took some time out from teaching geography
and made us sit down and discuss what we wanted to do.

Gareth for that was his name,
before he let his job become his life,
said he had no idea,
but he would be famous,
well known and for people
to be fearful every time they met him.

He did well enough at school,
came top in science,
but his grades in English were appalling,
the teachers said he had no talent
and words would not be his calling.

He had a dark robe
and a scythe,
and took up an apprenticeship,
alongside Old Father Time,
who liked Gareth for his energy
and his enthusiasm,
but not his complaining ways.

Everybody fell out with Gareth.
He was bringing in more money
and had a different girl on his arm
every night.

He said power was an aphrodisiac,
but now he wanders around from party to party
never being the life and soul of it,
instead taking them for his own amusement.

I have fallen out with Death.
He was alright once,
but now he just sits and scowls
and curses the luck he had.

I don't want to get on his wrong side,
but I fear that I might
one day, his work will cross my path
and people will say Death is just Nature's way,
but I will know different.

Death could have been anyone,
but it is Gareth,
a sad, bitter man.
who was given the
wrong type of career advice.

Ben Macnair

Waste Not The Time

And now, what shall we say
To all the dust of ages past
Who strove in vain to see our day,
Their kings and queens of royal blood
Were born and raised as you and I to live
Then pass away, forever, and for good,
Time now does thumb historic page
Our future yet unborn does sleep
The waiting fruit of this our tubal age,
Not all shall see the glorious days ahead
Tomorrow's stage is not for them
Alas, their mortal armour now is shed,
Should this dark morning be our last
Through finger'ed hearts our living sand runs out
Our precious time to waste is passed.

Terence Powell

The Beach

A sea of faces, never once the same
Ever changing flows flux
The babble bubble of voices
Weaving whorls where eddies snare
Islands form, dissipate, reefs rise
With undercurrents of mood
Shoals shift and shimmer
Carrying melancholia in the midst
Of where rhythms rise and fall
With the click-clack percussion
Music accidental harmonies
Discordant thoughts of broken orbits . . .
Here a cold wave submerges me
Unities are illusions
Sea mirages formed of the flotsam and jetsam of souls
Washed up here like driftwood, drying and lost
Sparkling with sea salt in the sun
Seized unresisting, by the tide
Different, but all hopelessly the same
Tormented by the raw viscous undertow
Denying safe havens here
No storm-safe moorings
I could cry out loud
But would not be heard
Only stared at temporarily
Furniture forces patterns regularity
Aisles channel human currents
In and out, in and out
An irresistible tide
Here lurks regularity dead but fed
By this human flow predatory
Human thoughts, like hungry sharks
There is no unity, only chaos, inescapable
No safe havens, no comfort
Dragging anchors torture because . . .
All that is solid melts into air
All that is solid melts into air
All that is solid melts into air.

David Denny

Life

When you're a child life's full of fun,
Playing with your friends until day is done.
Then it's straight off to bed, counting the sheep,
Until at last you fall asleep.

When you get older, into your teens,
Nobody cares or so it seems.
Rebellious, you're always right,
You'd even argue that black was white.

Then when you're an adult,
You receive the key to the door.
What all that means is you're not really sure.
For you've done all the things that the law now says you can,
Now you're an adult, a woman or man.

As quick as a flash, you're middle-aged,
A few aches and pains at the end of the day.
Your once vibrant hair is turning grey,
You're set in your ways, the groundwork is done,
Hoping in future you can relax in the sun.

Then you retire, the time has finally come,
When the only marching you'll be doing
is to the beat of your own drum.
You reminisce the past more often than not,
Remembering the times you thought you'd forgot.

As the years go by you don't seem to care,
That just around the corner your Valhalla waits there.

Finally your eyes close, once again you count sheep,
Until at last . . .
Eternal sleep.

John A Turner

A Ballad Of Nelson

A man of his time and one of the best
With a single eye and a one-sleeved vest,
Nelson's at sea and away to the west,
Aboard the oak of old England.

On sighting the French and the Spanish too,
He hoists a signal without more ado,
With the Temeraire in lines of two,
Aboard the oak of old England.

They struck the foe where it hurts a lot,
Through the stern, with red-hot shot,
The killing was grim but they cared not a jot,
Aboard the oak of old England.

In the heat of the battle there he stood,
Thinking of Emma and whether she would,
Till an enemy let out his blood,
Aboard the oak of old England.

In a cabin dim, he spoke his last word,
'Kiss me Hardy,' then a silence occurred,
As his spirit soared on a great white bird,
Aboard the oak of old England.

The statue we see in Trafalgar Square,
Was erected by us to an Admiral fair,
A breed of man growing all too rare,
Aboard the oak of old England.

Owen Davies

Poetry . . .

The time and space,
a peaceful, calm and quiet place,
here in Nature's salvation,
is writing's redemption.
Cosmic forces flow through and within.
Rivers of sunlight through my mind.
Inspiration does begin . . .
Like gossamer strands of wonder,
A web of imagination is lit.
Earth's gravity creates through me,
Words unite and a story is writ . . .
Comes writing from what inspires
In natural beauty, everywhere it fires.
Whispered on a summer's breeze,
Or in colours that dapple the ground through trees.
Life is poetry.
On gentle wave of waters
Diamond light gleams;
Caught in twinkles of countless sunbeams.
In a new day's dawn.
For where rises our star,
New beauty in ideas are born.
For the world is poetry in motion;
As vast as space and deeper
Than any ocean . . .

Paul Holland

Wedlock Woes

Ambitions and dreams are one thing
Jostled around safe but sound now
It's all roaring and suffering when my
Wedding farce finally comes around, it
Wasn't my first time dear reader, I'm
not a young chit of a girl, I'm a mature
Aged something who got possessed by
A suitor in a whirl, I'm stranded in
This marriage, *'Damn it, I shouldn't
have said yes,'* washing baggy underpants and
a second off white vest, in the dauntless
Task called wedlock, I'm bold, intelligent,
I thought, greatness was inside of me till
My freedom and I got caught, I thought
I would be choosy, my hero doesn't exist.
Now I'm buying boxer shorts plus unmentionables
On my list, it's only been a fortnight honeymoon
that's a laugh, aches, complaints take over and
I'm slouching in the bath. Underhand plots
are called for, if I'm to survive these vows someday
I will be a lady, friends if you could see me now.

Angela Allen

Leek

This old market town called Leek
Set in the Staffordshire moorlands
With old ancient churches to worship in
All have features quite unique.

The market stalls still going strong
From way back in King John's Charter and reign
Anything you may wish to purchase
Or browse among all day long.

Down St Edward's Street you will walk
Black and white buildings, sturdy and strong
Look up to the roofs, high, tall chimneys
Have a meal in the café, sit and talk.

Antique shops, full to the brim
Buy an antique on your day out
Beautiful French furniture you can find
But in small, modern house it just wouldn't fit in.

I live in the country, out of the town
A village called Meerbrook, peaceful and calm
I have to go shopping once or twice a week
But I love a visit to our old market town.

Margaret Goldstraw

The Day The Stranger Came

I lived in the inner city,
Where life was grim and bleak,
With muggings a daily occurrence
And at night gangs roamed the street.

Now I'll tell you a tale and a strange one,
Though I'll take no praise or blame,
That the life we knew was changed overnight
On the day the stranger came.

In the daytime we lived in fear
And we walked down the street with dread,
You passed someone with a fleeting glance,
Then you kept your eyes ahead.

At night you did not go out
And you locked and barred your door,
And you did not trust your neighbour
And you told no one what you saw.

Now I was the first one to see him,
As I walked down the street to the shop,
As he passed me by, so he caught my eye
He smiled and I came to a stop.

My heart, it beat like a hammer,
My guts churned up inside,
It felt like the gates of Heaven
Had been laid open wide.

And I could not speak and I could not move,
Though I tried with all my might,
I just stood there like a lovesick fool,
While he walked right out of sight.

When I found that I could move again,
After him I ran,
And though I searched the streets all afternoon
I could not find that man.

And in my heart I felt a loss,
Like someone loved had died,
Like something great had passed me by
And I was left to bide.

And so I turned and went back home,
To sleep and dream awhile,
Of all the love that I had seen
Within that stranger's smile.

I awoke to a knocking on my door,
My neighbour he stood there,
Upon his face was a big, fat smile,
In his eyes was a glassy stare.

'I've seen an angel, mate,' said he,
'And believe me 'cause it's true.'
'Oh I believe you friend,' said I,
'For I have seen him too.'

And my spirits soared within me,
As I looked out at the street,
For people walked and talked and laughed
And kids played at their feet.

The night gangs disappeared
And the muggings they ceased too,
The church it was so packed at the weekends
They had to form a queue.

For all had seen the stranger
And all had felt his love,
It was a prize beyond all price,
A gift from Heaven above.

And I knew that on this side of death,
I'd not see him again,
For he left behind a peace and love
To replace fear and pain.

Some say that he was God Himself,
Though me, well I'm not sure,
I only know I'd sell my soul
To see his face once more.

Now we look to a brighter future,
Things will never be the same,
For our lives were changed forever,
The day that the stranger came.

J Card

Seaside Out Of Season

The seaside town seems to sit and wait
The *closed* sign swings on the café gate
The dull, grey sky shows that winter's here
And the crowds are gone from the wooden pier

But the tide continues to ebb and flow
The sun just waits for the clouds to go
The gulls will swoop by the beach once more
And visitors into the town will pour

Meanwhile, the gardens are being planned
There are men busy tidying up the sand
There's a smell of fresh paint in the air
And a happy feeling everywhere

So now there are children on the beach
The gulls are starting to swoop and screech
The café is full, there is bustle and noise
With the joyful shouting of girls and boys

But the season will finish and quiet descend
No one will walk on the pier, to the end
Again the town will sit and wait
And the *closed* sign will swing on the café gate.

Maureen Butcher

My Dearest Betsy

Her eyes are as blue as the summer sky,
She has a stare of a thousand dreams.
Skin as pink as a ripening peach,
As I help rub on her creams
She stretches out on the golden straw
And more awake by now.
I stroke her head on a soft warm bed,
My close to farrowing sow.

Richard Vernon

Plastic Floor Tiles

Plastic floor tiles and chrome door handles
Mean so much to me
This is my life every day
Seems like eternity

Plastic floor tiles and chrome door handles
Does anyone care
The windows high, up and out of reach
Cannot see out, I can only stare

Plastic floor tiles and chrome door handles
I see them every day
Will someone get me out of here
This I daily pray

Plastic floor tiles and chrome door handles
Mean so much to me
If only they could speak
They are my only company

Plastic floor tiles and chrome door handles
How are you friend?
For many years we have been together
We may be to the end

Plastic floor tiles and chrome door handles
I do not know what to say
I'm feeling tired and have to go
Please think of me and pray

Plastic floor tiles and chrome door handles
Let no one else suffer here
All I wanted was to smell the grass
And see the sky so clear

Plastic floor tiles and chrome door handles
I want to shout out loud
Thank the Lord at last I'm free
Floating on a Heavenly cloud.

L G Thomas

The Doctor's Room

I sit outside the doctor's room, inside I wish to go,
To hear the results of a test I've had,
Then the illness and cure I'll know.
Will it be just a common cold or something serious to worry about?
This worries me enough to feel the need to shout.
For I know there are illnesses that there are no cures for.
Not knowing what is wrong with me makes me so insecure.
I look into my doctor's face to see if I read what's there,
He looks back at me with a worried, concerned stare.
My thoughts fly around my mind, please say this news is not bad,
For it will make a drastic change to this precious life I've had.
The doctor's result is cancer, I feel like dropping to the floor,
I'm told the help that's on hand and the treatment that's in store.
I walk from the doctor's room, not knowing where to turn,
There to tell my loving family at home that there's cause for concern.
We sit down all together, the news to them I tell,
How would you react? Just think of the sheer hell.
Would you just sit there calmly and take this news with ease?
For on hearing you have cancer it can knock you to your knees.
Since hearing I have cancer
All we can do is fight the disease together,
For life doesn't run smooth you know,
There has to be some stormy weather.
If we can beat cancer then we are the luckiest by far,
Because cancer has no favourites it doesn't care who you are.
We all are not immune to this terrible disease.
It can come like a thief in the night
And take someone when it leaves.
One thing we can do is show cancer who really is the boss,
As it hurts so much to see someone whose battle they have lost.

Mandy Barrow

The Function Of Our Gossip

The table laid with silverware
The candles brightly lit,
A pastel posy centrepiece
Eight guests around did sit.
What subject did the talk now take?
Good humoured smiles abound,
A little banter on the side,
Discorant note may sound.
How do we all reach harmony?
Talk about some others!
The village scandal of the week
Is two new single mothers.
And if I take off for the loo
What will they say of me?
My fear I know's well founded
Detecting hand on knee!

We overcome our differences
By ridicule and pride,
Pointing out another's faults
Let's keep our distance wide.
We form community around
Out tittle-tattle times,
A scapegoat takes our hate away
And leaves us free of crimes.
Together we're against something
As governments well know,
A new Sadam or Hitler found
And off to war we go.
The function of our gossip is
The glue that holds us tight,
In thoughtless unity we act
To start another fight.

Mary Lefebvre

The Back Lane

At the top of my garden
There lies a secret world
And only certain people know
That it is waiting there.

Step through the cultivation
Around the cherry tree,
Behind the shed and compost heap,
A new world waits for me.

My wooden gate hides freedom,
From traffic noise and soot.
Shows off a world of secrets
With storage space for stuff.

Turn left or right no matter
Walk slowly down the track,
A leafy lane with hedges
No brambles there to hack.

Old buildings stand at angles
Coach houses, sheds and stores,
The perfect dens for children
To hide-and-seek and roar.

What joy to find such freedom
No need to weed, do chores,
Just to enjoy the nature
Keep off … no signs, no laws!

Lydia Talbot

His Last Race

The old fox lay in his lair 'neath the ground
As away in the distance he heard the baying of hounds:
He knew that again he must take up the race,
How often he'd challenged those hounds in the chase!
But now he was old and his limbs got so tired
When chased through the woods, the mud and the mire.
He knew full well he'd need all his cunning and power
If he was to survive the next critical hours.

As he weaved and he schemed the baying came nearer
And his old aching body was filled with great fear.
Was this his last race?
Had the years taken toll?
In the hands of the hounds was his fate, was his soul?

Then a miracle from nowhere appeared
A bright-eyed young fox drew up his side
And saw the tired eyes and the weary old frame.
He knew that this was a young fox's game.
He waited until the hounds got quite near
Then away from the old fox a course he did steer.

The old fox made his way back to his den,
He knew he'd been saved from the hounds, from the men.
Then slowly he laid his aching old frame
On the earth that was cool and dark and helped soothe the pain.
Then the tired old eyes in the rugged old face
In peace slowly closed, he had run his last race.

A Woolley

Living In The Dark

(Anne Frank Two years in the secret annex)

Today's stink of kale
is something I choose not to dwell on
though it's pungent enough
to enter the seams of our bedding.

These last months
I have grown breasts
held hard under my clothing
which no one but myself
seems to notice;
I am glad that at last I'm a woman
who menstruates
(though there's the awkwardness)
whose delight is in books
and who eats soup -
lately lettuce, mostly rotten
with barely the hint of an onion -
without complaint.

That same flutter of risk
as I peeped out last night between raids:
the real world, still there
rain, lovely and luminous.
How we long for invasion.

For a while I thought less of the rats
who are hungry like us;
I remembered the tree trembling silver,
the wet-weight of blossom.
Gifts from a force which knows nothing
of war.

Marilyn Gunn

Little Boy Blue

Just a child who is growing
I don't know who I am
Open fires are still glowing
Stay away if you can
My secret world is calling
I think I'm falling from the wire

Just a child who is weeping
Tears that fall into space
Golden slumbers for sleeping
Never come to this place
Nightmare dreams are waiting
Anticipating screams from Hell

Pretty maids all in a row
This little piggy stayed home
When the bough breaks I know I will fall
Wish I could follow the sun
Hide until morning has come
Little Boy Blue come blow your horn

Just a child who is bleeding
Wonder when I'll be leaving
Shadows fall on my pillow
Weep along with the willow
God I feel older
There is a cold wind through my bones tonight

Cow will jump over the moon
Jack will fall down all too soon
Wish I could run away with the spoon
All the king's horses and men
Couldn't put me back again
Little Boy Blue, come blow your horn.

Keith Forrest

There But For The Grace Of . . .

It's early, the fire is out as I sit in my armchair.
Hearing the milkman outside the door, I shout
Hope he will knock and say hello,
Even if it's just for the money, I don't care.

Telly blares away . . .
Programme after programme.
The cat sleeps, too hungry to play, my only friend,
Hope someone cares for her when she's old and grey,
But these days doesn't seem to be the trend.

I look out of the window and stare . . .
At the weather, at the people passing by
All oblivious . . .
Their heads full of their own worries and cares.

Telly still on, Scamp doesn't move,
What's wrong with her? The little dear.
Hey! What was that? Oh, it's the rent man tapping on the window.
Surely not a month gone by since he was last here?
No bin able to get out to draw me pension, so no money for him I fear.

Now there's a bang! Someone's breaking in!
Well, if it's burglars they won't find owt,
Not even money for the leccie bill,
All I have is my treasured wedding ring,
From my dear late husband Phil.

'*Grace!* It's the police *Grace!*'
Men in uniform, surely not?
Why do they pull a face and even gag!
Stop shaking me and what you doing in my handbag?

'She's stone cold, must have been like this for days.'
'Cat too,' I hear one say,
'Poor love, no next of kin, how sad to die this way.
Not even a neighbour to come check with a spare key.'
Are they talking about me?

How strange, my body seems far away,
I feel a strange pull, I see my body all lifeless and grey.
There's a bright light! Ah! Bless, Scamp's here too,
'Phil! . . . Phil is that you? Why you look alright!'
My God! It is him, he's taking my hand . . .
Leading me away from my lonely plight . . .

And we all walk, going home at last, towards the love and light,
One last look at my empty body,
No one to care . . . Dying alone . . .
For anyone surely *that's not right*.

Deborah Harvey

Lorraine, You're Always On Our Minds

(So young lady, you have the right to be proud, just pin on your medals You will always stand out in a crowd. Lorraine, our granddaughter, oh boy are we proud. P.S. an old North Stafford will always be with you, love you always, Gran and Grandad.)

We nursed you as a baby, of you we are very, very proud.
We watched you as a child growing up with all the other kids around.
We watched all your school productions, you stood out in the crowds.
We saw you as a beautiful teenage, giving the boys the run around.
We saw you cope with both happy and sad times but you always made us proud.
We saw you as a teenager going through difficult times
But you always chose the right way, not the easy way around.
We saw you join HM Forces and with difficulty make that all important passing out parade.
We saw the determination, the guts and braveness, the stuff of which you're made.
We saw you on that parade quite a few years ago,
Of the emotions, the pride that swelled our hearts you will never know.
We had tears of joy, of happiness, lumps in our throats,
Oh yes, our hearts were swelled with pride.
We saw you go to Ireland, to Iraq as well and now Afghanistan
And we know again you will do it well.

Ronald Astbury

Tinnitus

I awake to the sound of turbulent waters rushing,
Downwards through a narrow mountain gorge.
Next comes the rhythmic tapping of hammers,
Echoing from an ancient blacksmith's forge.

Then what I can only describe as an angry swarm,
Of large bees, buzzing behind a windowpane.
Which is followed by the hissing of steam,
Blowing from an old locomotive train.

At last a period of peace and quiet, until I hear,
Some budding musician practicing on a violin.
These are just a few of the many irritating sounds,
That come from somewhere deep within.

It is of small consolation knowing that Goya,
Suffered from this appalling affliction too!
When I myself have been its victim,
Since the year nineteen hundred and sixty-two.

Norman Plant

Maiden Of The Waves

A maiden so fair
With the sun on her hair
And the sky in her eyes so blue.

You shield your eyes
From the glare of her eyes
And feel the warmth of the sun around you.

You look out to sea
Where the maiden will be
On the rocks being lapped by waves.

This maiden so fair
Is so very rare
That no one believes in her these days!

Lady Sandie Smith

Spring Is - When?

Farewell last fieldfares
waiting
by the Wye for a west wind?

The first bumblebee
feasting
after her long winter fast?

Early sandmartins
crossing
Africa for river banks
swooping for insects
cleaning
former homes for families?

Over brown bracken
singing
of the hovering skylarks?

On hearing the first
chiff-chaff
is spring. And daffodils shout.

V J Cleaver

Lost Love

All my life I will remember,
the memory may die,
the memory may lie dusty yet not forgotten by and by.
Sweet, gentle words spoken sincere with a love unbroken,
that smile, that look,
liken on to a lovely book in which a story of love was written about two people
whose hearts were smitten.

This memory will live as long as I,
and perhaps it will live on when I die.

John Winston-Smith

Walking With God

When you're walking with God
It's a wonderful thing
Just to know He is there
By your side.

When you're talking to God
It's a marvellous thing
Just to know that He cares
And you're satisfied.

As tall as the trees
That grace the proud land
You'll walk with your Lord
And He'll take your hand.

When you're walking with God
It's a beautiful thing
So lift up your hearts
Rejoice while you sing.

And He will pray
For you every day
When you are walking with God.

Ian Proctor

The Coach House, Laugharne

When the lone curlew
calls across the water -
when owls hoot
from the night cold black -
when wild geese speak
through the mist of early morning -
then the old Coach House at Laugharne
will call you back.

Christopher Mills

A Mother's Love

It takes a special kind of woman
To have a mother's love, that is true
For she is that one in a million
She is the one person looking after you.

For she will have a loving home
And care for your every need
With a mother's love you're never alone
For her devotion to you is guaranteed.

For a mother's love knows tolerance
As she brings up her family
For she is born with patience
Getting it right shows unity.

A mother's love is endless
Putting a child first with reassurance
Giving love with kindness
But most of all growing up with confidence.

A mother has wisdom
Has she learnt from her mum?
A mother's love has welcome
To which a child does succumb.

A mother's love has trust like no other
Guiding children through life itself
Pushing away pitfalls, this is a mother
For she is there in sickness and health.

Walter Mottram

My Space

How do I fill 'my space'?
Not the cyberspace kind
But the expanse of my days
in this time and place.

Will I look back, reflect
Feel the choices I made
Were unwise or delayed,
sense a sadness, regret?

What have I learned, achieved?
Who shares my life and loves
The deepest seed of faith
hidden and felt, believed?

Our thoughts are crowded out.
Work life strained and pressured,
Striving to halt the rush
of routine roundabout.

We've conquered outer space,
Now inwardly seek peace
And sense of truth and hope,
of spiritual release.

Well-being, peace and love.
To be free, hopeful, still.
These are the treasure found
in 'the Father's space' above.

Rachel Hall-Smith

For Lisa And Trevor

I am so proud of you my son
The way you've built your life
And there to support you all the way
Your lovely, lovely wife
I know times have been hard for you
To get your life on track
All I know it's wonderful
To know that you are back
We must forget the last few years
The heartache and the pain
It's worth restoring what we have
Now you are here again
My little boy with golden hair
And eyes as blue as cornflowers
My first born son, so special
And bright as summer showers
As well as my son, you are my friend
And you're with me in my autumn years
The world is sunny, and oh so bright
It's banished all my tears
There's no more I can say to you
My heart is full of joy
But I must remember you're a man
No longer my little boy.

Maureen Baxter

Where Have I Been?

(With thanks to Ann Cody)

A dark lonely place I found myself in
Didn't know where I was going nor knew where I'd been.
Living each day, so full of despair,
Who could I talk to? With whom could I share?

I plucked up some courage to summon some help
'Twas time to sort my mind, my life and my health.

About myself learnt things I never knew
Things about my past still make me blue.
Bullying myself, putting myself down,
Worry about others, forever wearing a frown.

Deep seated issues still make me feel bad
Day after day still driving me mad.

So what's next? What can I do?
My mind says to me, *time to think of you!*
Need to do more, start living my life,
Be more carefree, time to see the light.

Now slowly moving forward, step by step,
Doing little things to stop feeling a wreck.
Feeling more positive, cutting me some slack,
And that dark lonely place? I ain't going back.

Clive Hughes

That Fateful Day

It was a sunny September morning in New York.
Life as usual was busying itself in the World Trade Center.
We stared in disbelief
Was this really happening?
Two aeroplanes smashed into the Twin Towers,
The symbols of America's might obliterated for the world to see.
Two horrific acts perpetrated by fanatical terrorists in the name of religion.
These incredulous events shocked and numbed the sane world,
leaving an indelible imprint.
I silently wept for those poor souls,
helplessly trapped and terrified knowing their fate.
A woman was waving a white cloth, and people were falling from great heights
trying to escape the towering infernos.
Resembling a pyroclastic cloud of acrid smoke, the shroud of dust
quickly advanced suffocating countless numbers of innocent people.
So many died that day, a wave of sorrow shrouded part of our world.
As we stood reeling the enormity of those well co-ordinated acts,
instigated by sheep-like, misguided men indifferent to the sanctity of life,
our numbness gave way to smouldering anger.
Let us hope this does not burst into an uncontrollable hate,
that annihilates other innocent people.

Audrey Faulkner

Their Best Of Both Worlds

The playwright and his acolyte
Moved deftly on the floor
The drags they started cheering
Calling out for more
Sarah Jane saw Ruthie
And felt it in her eyes
Haunted by duality
They'd waited for that night
Les frères de zip were chanting
Above a head of stone
A cold and ghostly ritual
They'd learned one year in Rome
The acolyte did handstands
And waited for his pay
The playwright inked a telling line
And put his quill away.

Tenuous lives on the shady side
Dancing through the night
Something flashed above them
But no one saw that light
A camp portrait of Venus
Looked down upon it all
And Sarah Jane and Ruthie
Heard the loving call.

Pretty boy Jim came waltzing in
With a mirror in his hand
He sang a hymn to Narcissus
And the sisterhood of man
The chief drew nonchalantly
On a loaded cigarette
Then he sent out for a rabbi
And a small mosquito net
The playwright cast his eyes about
Looking for some meat
His state of amorality
It was long ago complete
Then they all took partners
Was it boys or was it girls
And Sarah Jane held Ruthie tight
In their best, their best of both worlds
In their best, their best of both worlds.

Patrick Fitzhenry

Alas, My Love

Through long dark hours of night I look for sleep.
My eyelids close but clench with thoughts of you.
A sob of pain, a plea to God for some relief
from throbbing memories that lie askew
remains unheeded, unresolved. And still they come,
those vivid images of hands, of mouth and eyes.
Your smallest movement, mannerism, smile
are everything I love.
I hear your voice inside my head, and cry
the special words you used for me,
each nuance, lilt, inflection, modulation, tone;
and ache to see you once again before I die;
and dare not dream in case you are not there.

Remember times we had! Oh rapture, joy, desire:
our senses pared antennae-like; aware
of every star in Heaven, each glowing rainbow hue
and silly call of cooing turtle dove.
Re-live some secret tryst, our arms entwined
with gentle kiss. Embraced, we find
a mutual closest, furthest, highest, deepest love
is ours; and yet again I wonder how or why we met
in wild compatibility.

Illicit love. Beset with guiltless guile,
half rushing headlong t'wards unbridled lust,
half trying not to join that world of subterfuge and shame;
Such passion surely only made for us -
not possible that others felt the same
completeness or such oneness. Oh so right
the happiness o'erflowing through our veins,
a wondrous fusion binding inextricably
to free us from mortality.

But thus it is; and ever was before us, doomed to tears!
The world knows well the heart's desires and fears
and knowing, turns its gaze away;
for judgement, passed on those of us who stray
from straight and narrow paths of light
makes lovers hide sweet memories in darkest night.

Barbara Young

The Land Of The Midnight Sun

Light prevails, it's unending, it's difficult to adjust to time but is it necessary in such a place?
Different shades of green from millions of trees clothe the mountainsides
and nudge one another into meandering rivers.
Perfect symmetrical images of majestic mountains reflect in glass-like lakes.
Snow clings to the peaks but the hot sun makes it release its grip and come tumbling,
powerfully spinning over craggy rocks and down waterfalls
in a race to reach the still waters below.
White water rapids roar and plunge into valleys. Rocks glisten in the sunlight.
Some roads undulate, hug the contours of mountains, can hide beneath miles of tunnels
and peep from beneath the high walls of snow that tower above my motorhome.
Travelling over passes and manoeuvring hairpin bends
can keep one's blood racing through one's veins.
Reaching one's destination there is instant relief, a great feeling of elation and exhilaration.
Sheer cliffs, on some days mystically hiding their towering summits,
hang over the fjords making everything beneath appear minute and insignificant.
The air caresses all, sometimes gently and then when
pushed between Nature's sculptured cliffs echoes and blasts defenceless stones before it.
Yet one is surrounded by wildlife.
Food in the rivers and fjords provides ample sustenance for dolphins, salmon and birds.
The forests are alive with birdsong.
A Norwegian spruce reaches out with its green fingers to stroke the air
and protect the family of wagtails nestling in her bosom.
Reindeer and moose are close to the roadside but one would not intrude on their privacy.
All appears silent at the Arctic Circle.
Here there are no trees, yet it is not a wasteland.
Beneath the snow, hardly plants struggle to survive providing shelter for the birds
that have made it their home for the summer.
Flowers prize themselves between the rock crevices and bloom triumphantly,
showing that small jewels do exist beneath the snow.
At Norway's highest pass I gaze towards the horizon,
it is not a flat plain, jagged peaks still rise up into the blue sky.
Virgin snow contrasts dramatically with the darkness of exposed rocks.

High roadside poles warn the unwary traveller of the dangers of this remote region.
Apart from two birds calling to one another beneath the sprigs of sparse vegetation,
all is silent and breathtakingly beautiful.
How I marvel at this much quieter and gentler pace of life.

Audrey Faulkner O'Connor

The Bulldog And The Poodle

The bulldog and the poodle met and started to argue quite bad
About who could open the back door first, a cunning plan each one had.
The bulldog thought he would win as he was big and strong
The door would be open in a trice, it wouldn't take him long.
The poodle on the other hand was a weak little runt
Who wasn't up to the challenge as he couldn't even grunt.
The bulldog tried his luck first and rushed up to the door
And grabbed the knob with his teeth and tried to twist it with his jaw.
But he couldn't get hold of it and he had to let it go,
He tried again several times for it frustrated him so.
At last he had to give up and admitted his defeat.
So they went to the poodle's home, surely him he couldn't beat.
The poodle went up to the door and scratched it with his claw,
His owner came straightaway for he'd done it often before.
The man picked him up and gave him a welcome pat,
For he loved him very much and the poodle said, 'That's that!'
When we have a problem it's not always wise
To go full pelt at it like a bulldog in disguise.
It's better to be a poodle with the gentle touch
And approach it carefully which can do so much.

Rita Hardiman

Faith

Had a conversation about faith
About what a difference it made,
On whether to fear God's wraith
Or be it a friendship repaid.

The angel and the spirit-guide
Are always with you,
Though it may be a bumpy ride,
They'll always see you through.

The world is not going to end
On the given date,
On the Lord you can depend,
Time to believe because it's not too late.

Jonathan Simms

A Lickin' Good Finger Lickin' Gravy Train

Gordon
Brown
is
upside
down.
With tongues poised at the ready, the country
now is lickin' good, like red-hot coals they're
heady. The footplate now it's got quite hot!
The whistle has been blown.
Like fat cats on a hot tin roof they justify the rot!
But now 'en masse' the train is rolling down recovery lane.
All parties know they've got to take a shovel full
of blame. Steam is hotter than gravy I fear, so lick
those fingers and have a good year!

Patricia Jeanne Hale

Trinity - Bell And Boots

The vagrant, it seems is homeless . . . by choice.
No love or care from parents - wife.
Hostels no answer in his case,
Official opinions of the State.
This man, not old, an artist, first rate!

I met this man once - well, maybe twice
On a special day, when to our town
He made his way, as many, walking from afar -
Like the magi, wise men, following a star!

The vagrant, his friends - once dressed in red,
Black boots, on his feet- which shone
As the bell, in his hand, which he rang
Loudly, for all to tell, of Christmas Day.
Come lads and lassies - to dinner in the hall
The man in red, his bell, did call!
Merry Christmas one and all!

The reception in the hall, warm as the colour red,
Warmth, love, turkey dinner with pudding, after -
The music, singing, presents, laugher!

The vagrant, homeless by choice -
Had come again - for this special day -
Walking miles, like others, along the way!
Not for this day - the matted hair, scruffy sway -
But brightness of eye, shiny face,
For this day - is like no other
Peace on Earth, brother to brother!

The vagrant, his clothes - shabby worn,
Trudges along, with battered bags -
Seeking shop doorways - to keep warm!
One of mankind others scorn.

Mavis Newell

Our Sonnet To Memory

Love is our poetry, our sonnet to memory
To forget or to remember or merely be.
To harbour a thought, but never hold back time,
Ours is but now, a second that could have been.
The colours of summer, red until conker
Blowing now the leaves, red and brown crumble away.
Sanctify in solitude of silence unsolicited, unbiased,
Unspoken handcrafted from God.
Tranquillity untapered as winter arrives
A light behind the door ajar
One sweet summer garden memory
Of love and fear along this dark path.
Silent voices cry out unheard
A flickering beacon of distant street lamp.
The solemnity of the graveyard in sublime summer tranquillity
As birds fly into memory divided
Ours is not eternal, like the wind rushing through the trees
Beside the crematorium we soulfully said goodbye
In the shadows amidst the grey, grey tombstones
The darkness of the midnight procession would never anger
Could never be bitter, but be forever at peace.

Barry Powell

Halesowen

Halesowen once was a very quiet place,
Just a little village, that's for sure,
Where on Sundays, the children would all come to Church
With a well scrubbed face - and most demure!

Miners 'cots' were dotted here and there,
And plenty of old pubs, too.
There was lots of room in the Post Office where
You could chat, while you stood in the queue.

Well run schools, and little corner shops,
A few more, as Halesowen grew,
You could walk down the lanes, past fields of crops,
Cattle and sheep, and orchards, too.

But modern Halesowen isn't like that now,
For *progress* has put a stop to that!
There are car parks and offices where you used to see a cow,
In the new Post Office, you couldn't swing a cat!

Well, though there are traffic jams, and pavements full of people,
There's a topic now, that binds us all together -
Though the roads are all congested, we can still observe the steeple,
While we chat amongst ourselves - about the weather!

Lucy Williams

Widow

I feel my life is a doughnut,
Quite solid around the edges, but with a bloody great hole in the middle.
Alone I carry on cleaning, washing, eating, even wine drinking.
I've joined a reading circle,
I've joined a writing group,
I play bridge twice a week
But still that hole remains
It's largest in the evenings and especially weekends
When everyone has family but me.
I have no relations here to either love or curse,
My son's abroad, Florida, California and Australia,
They ring me and sometimes even write
But it doesn't fill that hole
And nothing ever will.

Charmian Howell

Let's Celebrate

A grassy glade amid pine-scented shade,
Just the place to celebrate.
Perhaps a number of Indians with an aromatically spiced banquet
Or is it a garden fete?
Bunting strung between the trees gently fluttering in the breeze;
Tombola, shove penny, fortune telling, stalls a plenty.
Maybe two lovers about to become engaged,
What a place for this to be staged?
Sun shafts filtering between green trees
The sky a perfect Wedgwood blue, what bliss!
Some day, someone will take your celebratory tome
To read in such a place as this.

Irene Hinton

The Hairdresser's

There's a little boutique, on the far side of town
It's small and it's friendly, and never lets you down.
On Friday after a long busy day,
I trundle along to see what the hairdresser has to say.
There's always a cuppa, a chat and a smile
And often we sit and wonder awhile.
After washing and drying my hair
There's a snip, snip here and a snip, snip there.
In go the rollers one by one
Then the job is nearly done.
Under the dryer and a read of my book
Hoping soon I'll have a new look.
A comb and some lacquer and off with the gown
Must say it beats those posh shops in town.

Pamela Reynolds

Manhattan Lights

When the sun sinks down low in Manhattan,
Evening skies seem to turn pink and gold.
City folk hurry home in the twilight
As the street lights shine out in the cold.

When the lights from the sidewalk glow brightly,
Loves kiss in the hush of the lane.
Yellow cabs race along 53rd Street,
Couples stroll in the gentle spring rain.

As the moon rises over the City,
All the lights shine like Hollywood stars.
We'll hold hands in the glow of the lamplight,
And we'll wish under bright shooting stars.

Oh, the Manhattan lights are so pretty
They shine like the stars in your eyes.
Lovers woo in the park beyond midnight,
And the diamonds blaze out of the skies.

Richard Charles

I Cry No More

The time has come for all nations to join as one
and stop the consequences of this final act of destruction.

The time has come for all people to join together.
stand under one umbrella,
not mushroom-like in clouds of smoke
but like the rainbow
Jesus spoke about in days of old
when Christ His people told, 'Enough is enough.'

And so He sent a dove, a dove of peace,
a symbol to teach, for the people had gone too far.

Like Sodom and Gomorrah
our lives are built on greed and gain
we fail to see the acid rain
that kills the Earth, burns the forest,
or with one explosion seals our fate -
'Too late!' we then would cry.

We talk of green and pleasant land
only then to find we stand in fume-filled street
or feed insecticide into the soil where Man would toil
just to make the crops grow faster.
Only then we find disaster.

And not content we are Hell-bent to poison the great oceans.
We dump our waste with undue haste
to watch the seals lie dying, what is the point in crying?
And so one day we'll count the cost
not pounds or dollars we have lost but life itself.

Joy Grant

A Day In The Life Of Me

Day after day, I wake up just before dawn,
barely stifling an early morning yawn,
bleary-eyed, I start putting on clothes,
shall I put these items on, or just those?
Ready for breakfast I walk through the door,
I do this, because that's what it is there for,
Pouring the last of the tea down my neck,
what time is it? Let's have a quick check.
Mornings make me feel grouchy, irksome and surly,
why does each day have to begin so blooming early?
Running and sprinting like mad for a 94 bus,
oh Hell! I missed the bus and continuously cuss.
Here I am, waiting at the bus stop for ages and ages,
my temple throbs and aches as my temper rages.
About time, a miracle, as now my 94 bus comes!
Most of the seats are filled with miscellaneous bums.
I sit next to a scruffy loser, who smells of beer,
As a playful hyperactive kid loudly screams in my ear,
There's an odour of someone's foul cigarette smoke,
if I found out who it is, I'll give their eye a poke.
At last, the end of my cheerless joyless morning ride,
some peon steps on my foot, I exit the bus from the side.
Looking over at the park, to see what I can see,
I can see a stray dog spraying his DNA up a tree!
What a day for my car to be broken down and kaput,
the bus was crap, from now on, I get here on foot.
Here I am, working for the big boss in the sky,
'matching and dispatching' and tots at fonts that cry.
That is, weddings, funerals and baptisms, well at least,
it's quite a mad hectic life being a parish priest!

Christopher Higgins

Summer Visitors

I watched our summer visitors today,
Coming to say one last farewell
Before they fly away to, who knows where,
In Africa, to stay till we again can offer warmth.

Their little family raised in such a tiny space,
Fixed with such care into the angle of the eaves -
Swooping with daring speed, in haste they come
For one last look at their summer place,
With nursery, their hard work done.

I see them chattering with their friends saying -
'Come, the day is here when we must leave the
Cooling air and find the sun - but when your winter
Here is done, we will come back again.'

Be not afraid, I'll not disturb your summer home,
But wait till next I see your darting flight and
Hear your voice - and know that summer once again
Is come. See you next year!

Jean Elizabeth Lewis

The Parting

Lay not your hand upon my arm
Or speak sweet tender words to me,
Pin not a flower next my heart
Nor take a slow paced walk with me.

Never glance again my way
Do not smile or frown,
Keep your eyes, so warm and dark,
Cast down.

Don't take my hand if we should meet,
Upon a hot and dusty street,
Keep your distance, keep away,
We have nothing more to say.

Frances Neale

Unsung Heroes

No prizes,
No cups,
No medals to be won,
Just another day

Of grinding labour
To be done.
Never wish to be a king,
In sumptuous palace,
With his queen,
Just soldier on,

Unheard, unseen.
Never complain,
Never curse,
Knowing well,
It could be worse.

No prizes,
No cups,
No medals to be won.
Just quiet satisfaction

At a job well done.
No brazen trumpets
Herald their approach,
No hosannas
Cheer them on their way,
No riding in a gilded coach,
But Shanks' pony
Every day.
No eulogies, no epitaph,

No blue plaque on the wall,
No pious statues
Standing in civic halls.

No prizes,
No cups,
No medals to be won,
Just quiet satisfaction
At a job well down.

R I G Doody

Whispering Trees

I talk to the trees
And they whisper to me
Of days so long, long ago.
When childhood play
Made me love them so.

They remind me of days
When young limbs climbed,
While branches held tight
And childhood laugher
Made dull days bright.

They recall a best friend
Who climbed higher than all.
Too shy to tell me true
So carved a heart with our initials
And an arrow through.

Though sadly now passed away
His heart lives on in memory.
The tree still stands so tall and strong
And passes on his message of love
To other climbing young.

And so at eighty years of age
When the trees whisper to me
As the soft summer breeze
Gently caresses their leaves,
I talk to the trees

And remember.

Heida

Little Jesse-Lee

We have a sweet granddaughter
Who likes to play with water
And any mess on the floor
It's in the bin behind the door.

When she comes
To Cu to play
She rolls up the carpet
And puts it away.

Then out come the toys
Blocks on the floor
Dinosaurs marching
Out through the door.

And when I call out
'Is that a tree?'
'No,' she shouts
'It's me, Jesse-Lee.

I'm only two,' she says to me
'And I can climb the apple tree
Don't forget Granddad Cu,
My name is little Jesse-Lee.'

And as the sun is out all day
She takes me by the hand.
'Come on Cu, it's really grand'
We end up playing in the sand.

So now it's time to get her home
Its Jesse's time for bed
'See you tomorrow and thank you Cu
Lots of love from Jesse-Lee.'

TB Rees

The Passing Of Jock MacCree

The intimation clearly said
That Jock MacCree was truly dead.
I racked my brain his face to recall
But could not place the man at all.

Was he the tall red-headed bloke
Who used to shout instead of talk?
Or could he be the shy quiet fella
Who married Tommy Murphy's Bella?

And then at last it came to me,
Fine, well, I know big Jock MacCree.
I haven't seen him for some time
But still he was a friend of mine

And so I did myself up smart
And off I went with heavy heart
To say goodbye to my old friend
Whose life had now come to an end

And when I reached the crematorium
I tried to act with quiet decorum.
I looked to find a friendly face
But could not see one any place.

Then, in the rain as I walked home
Soaked right through to skin and bone.
My thoughts were on big Jock MacCree
And the pranks we played when we were wee.

Then suddenly my heart near stopped
All I could do was stand and gawk.
For coming up the street towards me
Was my old friend big Jock MacCree.

Who's in the coffin I cannot tell
But I'm glad my friend's alive and well.
It was a near thing just the same
And all because they shared a name.

Frances Taylor

21st Birthday

21 you say, are you sure this is true, seems no time since I was too
So much passed time is incomprehensible, so much care given is so commendable
You've listened to each word I've written; sometimes I believe you
were almost smitten
You've given me such confidence, been truthful, honest no pretence
At times no inspiration came, contained a blank inside my brain
I'd wonder if I'd ever cope, with nothing there I'd not much hope
And then a child would ask a question. Giving me that inspiration
So badly needed for my next verse, new writings cannot be rehearsed
A funny happening, a deep despair something one said, a child in prayer
Then automatically I would begin, to write from feelings deep within
My father sisters, brother too, all let me write and misconstrue
Exaggerating, just a little, that pen of mine is somewhat fickle
Other writings are right from my heart, sometimes tearing me apart
When the ravages of life are out, and splinters scattered all about
Computer doing overtime, and knowing words I must refine
I wonder if it would be better, to just give up and write a letter,
But I can't do that, can't be untrue, for my success is down to you
Can't live without you I must confess, so happy 21st to Forward Press.

Jackie Davies

Not So Cynical

Where did the years go, from the days of summertime dreams,
Skipping barefoot and walking through shallow streams?
Before we all know it our prime has all gone
And nothing but a downward spiral, how much fun.
So you think I'm a little cynical? Well, I wonder why!
Maybe all I have to look forward to is the day that I die.
But that's not me, hold on right there
I'm still full of life and can offer lots of wisdom to whoever wants it out there.
Reason for living where do I start?
Maybe when I wake up each morning and feel the beat from my heart.

Steve Allen

The Price Of Coal

I remember, I remember chimney pots, and grim.
Buckets on the fire, working clothes on line,
Sunday school and dinner, going to the mine.
Bread and dripping in the pan,
Toasting fork, chips and spam.
Paraffin in an old tin-can
Mommy cleaning spick and span.
All these memories I do cherish
Till the day that I will perish.
Memories, faces caught in time,
Coal house door, Britannic mine.
Tips of slag, mats of rag, pipes and fags
Milk and tab, lead and bread
Toast dried egg, man in black,
Old coal stack, manacle brass and open fire
Still the tips, on hills grew higher.
Happy memories of long ago,
Blackout windows, larch on door,
Valley scarred through ages past
For her coal, her coke and gas.

And now the mines have all but gone
But our memories still live on
What a price for coal we paid
Trucks on scales, being weighed
Miners' families, wages small
Still kept their pride through it all
And through the windmills of my mind
My mates, I see some left behind
Memories faces caught in time
Walking to the valley mine
And still the tips on hills grew higher
For coal was king and workman's hall
And to our valley who saw it all
And now the surface screen
Is a place to dream
God bless them, God bless them all
And the price of coal was a nations' call.
And still the tips on hills grew higher

Carve their names with pride
In the ever-changing tide
Across the sea of time
The men who worked the mine.

John Daniel Rosser

The Righteous

For the love of man, you,
In loveless reprimand.
Soothing, to Mesmer, sing salvation!

From land torn from day to night,
Fallow, from light to dark,
The tallow, thought, the sowed seed.

The vessel, be righteous, or be damned,
Torments the soul, the crown of thorns,
The Holy Grail, the love of Christ.

The Holy Spirit, betrayed,
Be righteous or be damned,
Bartered lies, the force, in debt

Laboured to Hosanna, night and day,
Barter to Babel, peace,
Vengeance let loose.

In innocence I mourn,
In paler, sallow expression,
In paler grey conception.

They are thoughtless in belief,
Hypocrites hypnotists! Thieves!
In debt, be righteous or be damned!

Kerri Moore

Solitaire

One is a lonely number,
Two is how it should be,
But God helps us remember
How life takes away
And suddenly you are left free.

Despair and solitude
Team up like a pair.
When going to work,
Is the highlight of your day.
Oh what ingratitude you feel,
For joy turned into sadness.
Now Solitaire is the only game that you play.

The ticking of the clock on the mantel,
And the wasted hours that fly away,
The days the weeks, the months and the years
Vanish, and you wish you could find a new day.
Then Solitaire was the game you used to play.

Hilarie Grinnell

The Sparrow

I like listening to the sparrow
Though his range is narrow
And nowhere near as lush
As that of the thrush.
In fact his solitary note
Seems to stick in his throat
Like a rusty hinge
As though he'd been on a binge.
Yes, I admire this plucky little bird
As he chirrups away
He doesn't give a damn about being thought slightly absurd.

George Cowley

She Is My Inspiration

(Dedicated to my dear friend Lavinia Bousfield)

She is my inspiration
No idle hands has she
She may not always get things right
Because not all things have to be

The challenge is in the trying
And she really does have a try
She always keeps an open mind
One seldom hears her sigh

She showed me I had a talent
She taught me how to draw
A portrait of a tiger cub
Of family and much more

We share a love of poetry
She really is quite good
She writes of friends and family
And her dear departed love

We met first whilst on holiday
On the beautiful Isle of Wight
Despite the years between us
This friendship felt so right

Many an evening we have sat
My husband and I
Delighting in her company
Her stories to enjoy

We've had weekends at her caravan
Enjoyed the beauty all around
How lucky for the pair of us
Such a friendship as ours was found

I really am quite lucky
Whoever would have guessed?
That I should have a friend like her
I truly am, quite blessed.

Denise Edmonds

Thoughts

Thoughts must be for the good of all.
Words without thought 'Lead to nowhere.'
Positive, productive thoughts bring peace.
Negative thoughts do not lead to Heaven.

Love, joy, peace. The fruits of the Spirit,
The spirit of Jesus dwelling within.
Love, the greatest force on Earth,
It overrides all negative behaviour.

So let your thoughts have substance,
Let not selfish aims abide.
Love the good of others always
Dwell in thy soul divine.

So words must be the product
Of thoughts for peace and love.
No thoughts behind your speaking
Then, harmful, negative fruits.

Learn words are products that can harm
A fire out of control
Harbour your words, with thoughts of love,
See the results of your caution.

Ralph Watkins

Moon Follows

Bright silver balloon
Invisible strung
Wherever I go
Moon follows along.

Roger Mosedale

Crabbing In Cromer

Crabbing in Cromer -
Shrimping in Sheringham,
Growing up in Norfolk -
Summer by the sea.

Memories of beach days -
Picnics on the yellow sand,
Rock pools and fishermen -
Summer by the sea.

Lifeboats and beach huts -
Shrimping nets and summer skies,
Sandwiches and sand in shoes -
Summer by the sea.

Cliff walks and donkey rides -
Swimming in the ocean blue,
Sheringham my youthful home -
Memories of long ago.

Mike Storer

The Stream

Gently the rippling stream doth flow
Beneath a sky of blue
Stream, oh stream where do you go?
I wish I only knew.

You are so quiet in your journey
Fish and ducks each one you know
Lovingly little flowers stay by your side
Moorhens in your banks do hide.

They all look upon you with pride
The willow tree shelters you from heat
When you were sad with you did weep
Where do you go? I wish I knew.

Irene Barton

Listen

I long for those that have hurt me, to learn the true value of emotions
To understand how fragile they are to those that believe in their expression,
their freedom
And a way to explain that, once they shatter into fragments, like glass they are hard to restore
I long for a life to call my own. Not to be chained to another person's ideals
of how I am to live
And a way to carry out my days without prejudice, because of who I am
and who I choose to be
A way to be truly myself and live my life fully
I long for joy to shout my name, for I have already felt and heard pain knocking
on my door
I long to shout out in ecstasy and to feel the electricity arc through my body,
from my fingers to my toes
And a way to take my time and feel it building up in me, so slowly it almost
borders on an ache
I long to rest my head on the pillow at night, and not feel so terribly alone
I long for the real warmth of another, to no longer have to imagine the love there
And a way to know for certain that it is real,
To escape the possible humiliation of once again making the wrong decision
I long for the opportunity to learn, to revel in the knowledge of understanding
what I can see and touch
And a way to brush my hands over a piece of art, a tree
A way to feel the air on my fingertips and feel the heartbeat in all
And a way to know that I will not be prevented form doing so, not anymore
I long to know why, why was I stopped, why my heart still aches terribly
And a way to tell people that I tried to do all of these things,
to make others understand
A way to say that I did not give up hoping,
That I needed the assistance of others to achieve my dreams, but it was not given
I long to tell others that I am not a ghost,
That you may not see what is inside of me, but my physical self is all present
I long . . . I simply long.

Lisa Burton

Internal Scars

Deception, betrayal, the injured party,
Descriptive terms for those affected.
The internal foundations of life crumble and turn to dust
A deep thought occurs is this the end of it?
The pain the loss, unfortunately self torture continues,
Unfortunate for the infected but true.
Marriage and divorce deserve mental health warnings
That state, that which does not kill us makes us strong.
Fortunately there is a strength to be gained
A lesson to be learnt for sure
Stay positive to negativity
Not negative to positivism.
Life can take anything you throw at it positively
What you give is what you get in good time,
Faith in positiviness.
Deliverance, tranquillity karma is inevitable
Thank you.
Mark it with a scar
Scared stiff.
Let down by the system
A compass is needed to contrive
Unhelped and unheard by myself.
Deliverance deserves acknowledgement
Correct, correct, correct,
Thank you.

Darren P Morrall

Time Bomb

Gobble, gobble, slurp, gulp, crunch, munch, gobble, slurp
Swallow, munch, gobble, slurp, crunch, munch
Drip, burp, slurp, swallow, crunch, dribble
Munch, gobble, slurp, crunch. Tasty lunch!
Exercise, what a drag, have a fag?
Huff, puff, cough, cough.

Sip, drip, slurp, crunch, sip, burp, chomp, munch
Sizzle, sizzle, chomp, chew, guzzle, swallow
Sip, spill, dribble, munch, crunch, burp, chew
Thick bread, hot stew. Have a fag?
No, have two! Cough, cough, snuffle, oink! Oink!
Rustle, rustle, chomp, munch, cough, cough

Oh my! Chocolate crunch, have some more!
Swallow, drip, slurp, slurp, nibble, nibble
Crunchy crisps, chewy toffee, chocolate cake, Mmmm! Mmmm!
Oh no! Guess what? All gone! Ate the lot!
Stomach ache, huff, puff, cough, cough, had a fright; I'm alright,
Where's my fag? Cough, cough. *Tick-tock, tock-tock*

Slurp, burp, swig, swallow, suck, chew, crunch, munch
Pies, chips, chicken curry, have some more, very nice
Chomp, swig, have a cig, cough, cough, cough, cough
Feeling sick, go to loo, I'm alright, how are you?
Tick-tock, tick-tock
What's next? Bring it through!

Sip, lick, suck, gulp, sucky sweets, have a few
Sausage roll, cream puff, have that too!
Fish and chips, takeaway, ice cream, fry up
Get the beer, there's a dear
Tick-tock, tick-tock
Watch the clock.

Chomp, chomp, crunch, munch, drip, slurp
Suck, swig, guzzle, burp, tick-tock, too hot!
Pain in chest! Can't breathe! *Bang!*
You know the rest,
Did our best,
Laid to rest.

Slither, slither pitter, patter, rustle
Rustle, lick, lick, bite, scratch
Tickle, tickle, gnaw, gnaw, suck, chew
Drip, drip, drip, drip
Shudder, shudder, wriggle, wriggle
Tick-tock, tick-tock, watch the clock
Now there's nothing left of you
Drip, drip, drip, drip, *tick-tock*
Tick -
tock . . .
drip!
drop!

Marie Francis

Footprints

I trace your footprints
To your door
In snow so deep
I trip
I fall
Just like the first time
That we met
A love so wonderful
How could I forget?
An icy blast yet to come
For winter found you
Your heart still numb
But if you trust
If you believe
That my feelings are pure and true
With just one touch
I melt into you
For winter's grip has been and gone
The frost thawing
Your heart my home.

Samantha Williams

A New Day

Peering over the horizon
Comes the early morning sun
Heralding the dawning,
That a new day has begun.

It paints a splash of colour
On a canvas of sky blue
With shades of yellow among clouds of white
And topped with a crimson hue.

As it rises in the sky above
And the colours slowly fade
It lightens the sculptures on the cliffs
The raging seas have made.

The grasses that bend under the heavy dew
On the hills and fields below
Sway, back and forth, like rows of pearls
As a breeze begins to blow.

The wildlife waken from their dreams
The flowers put on their show
And birds, their dawn chorus sing
Cheered by the morning glow.

And as the air begins to warm
By the heat from the rising sun
Once more we also waken to greet
The new day that has begun.

Leslie Frank Checkley

The Poet

The poet sighed wearily and laid his pen to rest
Upon the antique, oaken desk.
'Oh woe'. Such a blissful yet tiring voice.
He looked at the writing before him, inviting the hours he'd spent of his own acute worth.
Another ode completed to put on the shelf,
Fervently penned by the poet himself -
In the midst of this thundery night.
Ah yes. Such a pleasing result.
A satisfied smile stole his face for a while,
As the sweetness of brandy traced on his lips.
And he gazed at the rain through the dark windowpane.
'Such genius!' He sighed as he stroked at his words.
And he took up his book as the ticking clock struck . . . 3am.
The brandy glass down, he started for bed with more visions to draft in his head.
For poetry -his love, his ideal -was there in his thoughts lying dormant, romantic,
But now yet to sleep.
And the newest of scrawl lay fresh in his drawer,
With a depth of passion to be gilded and shown.
And the pen from where the concepts stemmed, lay restful in the storm -
Still warm,
From the poet's hand.

Lynda Ann Green

Walk With Christ

(Recalling Rebekah, two years old, gripping my hand and whispering, 'Come play hide-and-seek Nanna, find Ha'b'en.' Watching my face for assurance as we tiptoed exaggeratedly from room to room, I glimpse the closeness of trust God wants from us. Xmas 2008)

Come child! Come walk with Me.
Let's ford the streams and cross the rocks,
And realise our dreams.
Climb mountains high we slip and slide
And fall upon our knees.
Let's reach for one stage further up
Than you can yet conceive.
Let's face the dark of blackest night.
One cautious step at a time.
Ne'er knowing what each step will bring.
Your hand held tight in Mine.

Let's face the winds of tortured storms
And shiver in the cold.
And wade through drifts of freezing snow
Towards our Heavenly fold.

Let's tramp down paths through arid plains,
Their thirst and hunger share.
And loneliness encompass,
When no one seems to care.

Let's press through crowds of angry folk
Hard pressed by guilt, stress, fear.
The wounds of this world
Making life so hard for them to bear.

And then My child you'll stronger grow
As you depend on Me.
I'll guide you safely through this life
Till Heaven's gates we see.

Then home we'll come, rejoicing loud
True peace now to obtain.
In Father's waiting, open arms
Where you belong again.

Then you will know each step you took
You took with me beside.
So that each problem we did face,
We took it in our stride.

Christina Fowler

Good Poetry

I have been reading a classic poem
That does use words that are obtuse
No way my simple mind could know
I simply haven't got a clue.

Like listening to tone poem music
No rhythm, harmony or tune
One has to pretend to listen
Or the others think you a fool.

Like a surrealist picture
Paint without meaning or form
As a jigsaw by idiots
A picture I would never have bought.

So the secret to writing good poetry
Is not to try to be clever
But to write something people understand
Something to give them pleasure.

W Stevens

Because I'm Sad

Don't look upon this face today
For sadness shows and deep despair
Don't gaze upon my face today
For my true self, it is not there
Today I need to hide away
To find my peace of mind
So do not look at me today
If you would be so kind
When I am glad and worry free
Then I would ask you to look at me
And see the joy within my soul
Yes look at me, now I am whole.

Jacqueline Claire Davies

Bridges

Love lies bleeding
On this human battlefield
For there is no conceding
As right will never yield
The human seed is planted
Wild amongst the weeds
For every mind that's ranted
Knows that all life bleeds
Too soon our journey ends
Will we ever know the way
To follow a road that bends
For the butterfly's just a day?
Yet we can all build bridges
That fail to cross the road
That end in forehead ridges
Yet fail to ease the load
Can we not be like the bee
Moving from flower to flower?
Life could be so easy
Savouring each hour
Yet love needs a leech
To draw liquid from its womb
So that all and each
Live from cradle to the tomb.

Cedric Thrupp

It Is A Shame

'Little robin why are you standing there?
You should be flying in the air
I know it is windy and it is cold
But as a robin you should be bold.

So little bird take to the wing
Let me once again hear you sing.'
The robin replied, 'It is very hard
When you are on the front of a Christmas card!'

Brian Harris

Have A Care

The day will come
When we see no more
Birds of prey as they swoop and soar.

Butterflies floating on the summer breeze,
Squirrels playing in the trees,
Whales blowing,
No more slaughter.

Icebergs glistening in frozen water,
Polar bears treading on thin ice
With little ones following,
Oh so nice.

We don't know the cost
But this is the price.
The world keeps turning round and round
We can't stop this clock,
But we *can* slow it down.

William Shire

Work In Progress - Barcelona

Here is the cradle of the chisel.
The womb of the fractured stone.
Grotesque and strange the figures hang,
and necks crane back and back
to ponder.
Who knows what nightmares, visions,
fuelled the desires of Gaudi.
Angels and demons throng his dreams,
unfulfilled.
Waiting patiently, the cathedral
hovers halfway from Earth
to Heaven, in the curiosity
and wonder of this tourist's mind.

Janet Harmer

Heaven Street Blues

Won't you come along with me
to the heavenly city?
We're on the road to the Promised Land.
Walk step by step by faith as God has planned.

Past saints surround us,
Jesus Christ will greet us,
Make the path level for your feet
onto Heaven's street!

Going home! Not alone.
Seek the way, now, today!
Don't shrink back, or get slack -
Consider Him who suffered so,
and don't lose heart or weary grow.

Fix your mind up above;
hold fast hope, faith and love.
To the place - our heavenly home.

Kate Arkell

Tsunami

Far from their frozen homeland
The young lovers strolled with hands entwined
Along a tropic shore, in all joy and innocence
They left their footsteps there.
Far out to sea and deep, deep down
A repressed Earth fermented
It boiled and raged with mighty force
And in anger, spewed out a monster wave
The lovers stared in awesome fear
And clung together tight
But its force would not relent
As on and on it came, its torrent drowned the shore
Till at last its wrath assuaged and all were washed away
It slunk back to its ocean lair to lie in wait once more
Then two white doves rose and flew away
To a happier land.

Doreen Gardner

To Mom

(An ode to Mandy Sue, aged thirty-five)

My life has had its ups and downs
Right from the very start
But I have known life's happiness through
Your love though miles apart

Your daily calls and little notes
And trips out in the day
Have left me with the memory
Of your loving special way

You often came to visit with
A potted plant or two
I wasn't much of a hostess
But then you already knew

I didn't ask for much in life
My cottage, cats and flowers
Just somewhere quiet and peaceful
To while away the hours

But then life dealt a wicked blow
Of hurt and stress and pain
But you were there to help me out
To lean on once again

I fought it out, was brave and strong
Although I had no choice
You were always there to talk to me
With your kind and tender voice

You nursed me through the last
Nine months, put me before all others
That's why your love has seen me through
The love of yours my mother

I do not know what lies ahead
Only what has gone before
But I know your love will see me
Through, of that you can be sure.

Pam Jeames

Six Little Darlings

Janet and Sue
Born together as two
Janet, quiet and petite
In her little shell she goes
Sue on the other hand
Comes across all shy
And doesn't trust anyone
Once you pass the test
You will see her at her best
Ruth and Wendy
Born together as two
Ruth is bubbly, dizzy and childlike
Wendy is a gifted artist
Her art is still in her head
Instead of putting it down on paper
Hazel and Caroline
Hazel is a social worker
At work as well as home
Cares for everyone and for her son
Caroline is the same
She's the nurse in the family
Like Hazel she's got a good heart
Both firm but nice with it
They are all beautiful people
Each one has something different to give
It's an honour to know you all
Me, myself I'm only four foot eleven tall
When I am with them I feel six foot tall.

Kim Gourlay Almey

Forest Fare

Wooded refuge in the Forest of Dean
Stillness and quiet it should have been,
But as I relax in this leafy glade
My ears are invaded by sounds man-made.
The overhead drone of lofty planes
And river-boat splutters as if in pain.
Daytrip children crying, 'More ice cream!'
And distant motorway buzz road planners' dream.
So I let my mind wander, back one hundred years
Imagining this scene of oak, sycamore and firs,
Of a forest at ease and gently sun-kissed
A tranquil yesteryear now vanished in the mist.

Gary Lanham

None But The Brave

The coxswain steers the lifeboat
With the trust of the brave crew
Racing against tides so strong
Over rocks and sandbanks no longer in view

Huge waves that form a wall of water
Up and down, rolling side to side
Saving lives against the odds
The willing face the task with pride

Returning home to families ashore
Until the next time worry is no more
Others will follow as crews get older
The endeavour no less the bolder.

Brian Bates

Haunted

My father was a mining man - and all his three brothers too
Sharing a 'stall' all their working life - luckily all came through.
He went down the pit at twelve years old - came up at sixty-five,
Battered and careworn, tired and old, but glad to still be alive.

No pit baths then - just a tin affair in front of a roaring coal fire,
Or out in the brew house to go scrub his back, of this I'd quickly tire.
Like an underground map, traced over his back, blue lines, little and thin,
Scratched, crawling through passageways the coal dust with healed over skin.

The frightened sad eyes of a twelve-year-old, the haunted look of his dad,
Knowing no other life for him - his protection all his dad had.
Sharing the darkness, the stench, the fear; hewing black gold till he bled,
Then a rush of cold air, sudden thundering coal a murmured sigh,
'Someone's dead!'

The dreaded call, villages abuzz - haunted, shawled wives at the pit,
Each huddled figure with a prayer in her heart please, not mine who's been hit.
Aching suspense, long hours seem like days not knowing but fearing the worst,
A sudden roof fall? A cage dropped too fast? - then for some the
searing tears burst.

We knew times were hard, cash always short, few clothes, no holidays, no cars.
To blot out the pain with brothers-in-arms, men often found solace in bars.
Too often in drink and fighting their mates, trying to forget their hard lives,
From fleeing families we heard stark tales, we all knew 'battered wives'.

Changed by time passing, new methods new machines, union protection
all round,
This glorious new world for which they had fought, better value now
for the pound.
But needs change and people do too - once esteemed values erode over years.
For our heritage, our pride, the generations to come, forcefully we now
voice our fears.

Carrie Summers

The Servant Said

The servant said she hates the ashes
and the bowing in the rags
to no one.
But up the narrow backstairs
without the dancing banister
or the pretty useless pictures
she'll pretend they never happened:
'Bring me some wine!' or
'Shall I accept Lord Whoever?'
Hoping that only the draught will hear
as it makes friends with her warmness.
Under the low ceiling,
she'll sit in silk and stubbornness,
on the tatty, hard, unposted bed,
dreaming away the dinge.
Stop it girl - there's no time to be still -
which of the bells is ringing?
(And they all could do with polishing.)

Matthew Thomas

Unless

Unless a grain of wheat falls into the Earth and dies . . .

God I seek You through dejection,
may my dejection serve You.
I seek You through grievous loss,
may my loss serve You,
connecting me more deeply
to the mystery of the Cross,
of Easter dawn,
key to the Eucharistic feast,
making us whole and free
to accept and value more deeply
Your amazing mercy, God of love.

Angela Cutrale Matheson

Our Beauty In Miniature

The beauty of a rose in bloom
As summer comes to call
The sound of nightingale's sweet song
O'er hedge and garden wall
The flash of blue by rippling stream
Reminds me dear - of you - and
That's what brings memory of
The things you say and do
The pink of summer's fairest flower
Is like the flush of dawn
The tune of summer's melody
Is like a song reborn
The blue of birds' rainbowic hue
Reminds me of your eyes
So lovely - all in miniature
They really light the skies
And as the day deserts the morn
And gives to all such peace
That's when my thoughts
Come back to you
And gives my heart - release.

Joan Winwood

Holidays

Those big aeroplanes are taking off into the sky
As people on the ground are waving family and friends goodbye.
They've kissed and embraced and said, 'Have a good flight.
And please, please, please don't forget to write.'
They are going to exotic places for their holidays
Where they can just do anything for days and days and days.
Like sitting on a nice big stretch of golden sand
With a long cool drink close to hand.
Writing postcards to their families back home
Who wish they were out there, instead of being alone.
But once their holidays are over they will surely recall
What a fabulous time was had by all.

Ruth Warrington

A Snip Of Fashion Past

1980, adorned in a jumpsuit, a jacket in black,
A Purdy style haircut, it just took a knack.
Dressing different was best a challenge to the rest,
Stand out in the crowd, set the trend and be proud.
1980-90, hairstyle's spot on, new romantics frills and lace,
Brightly coloured make-up adoring every face,
Ra ra skirts and frilly shirts, the gender was hard to tell,
Creating fantastic hairstyles with hairspray, mousse and gel.
1990, long flowing skirts with little flattie shoes,
Avidly watching Diana as she appeared on every news.
Chanel style suits, gold buttons and tiny bows,
Dogtooth checks from one's head to one's toes.
1990-99, leggings at last assigned to the bin,
Lace, silks and black leather are once again in.
Tighter and shorter with bits hanging out,
See-through in everything, so much flesh flashed about.
Easy to dress with much less to wear,
If the sun always shone we'd be walking around bare.

Josephine Sylvia Huckvale

You

And oh, how you make the world work.
All the everything is alive,
electric fizzing;
underneath your eyes
air is thick
and my voice struggles up.
Half-smile curls my stomach,
shallow breathing,
secret mind held snapshots
will remain.
Wonderful, fleeting you.
Heart thumper and fingertip touch shocks.
Everything is new.

Naomi Portman

Dream Or Vision?

Was I awake or in a dream last night
When I beheld the keeper of foresight
Who led me to a vast continent where
One stood skyscrapers high into the air?
Now devastation reigned from shore to shore
Prosperity and progress were no more.
Buildings were crumbled fine as sifted sand
Still was the air and barren was the land.
There was no birdsong, whistle call or bell
To call to dawn, to work or e'en to prayer
All was obliterated once was there.
With tear-filled eyes I asked him to explain
This gross destruction, queried the victor's gain
Then I beheld would be aggressor's state
It too lay useless, lifeless, desolate.
And so it was of all that lay between
Earth scorched, parched, where once were pastures green,
And seas and rivers boiled before my eyes
Clouds of steam eclipsed the stars and skies.
The Earth on its own axis reeled and turned
And its own solar orbit strangely spurned
And forward raced, ten times the speed of light
As if Hades had hailed it, in its plight
Then when its scorching race our Earth had run
To this grey planet Earth became a sun.
And when our Earth as sun did shine sometime
On that cold planet of ice, rock and slime
Slim creatures of a vaguely human form
Squirmed, crawled, stood, walked.
World ended, new world born.

Jane McGloin

Thyme

I think that age is in the mind
Sometimes good, sometimes unkind.
Born as babies, fun and happy,
Motherhood harass and snappy.
Holidays and school time years,
Growing up laughter and tears.
Time for us to come of age
Twenty-one years - now turn the page.
Midlife crisis sometimes happen
Older age, now forms a pattern.
Live each year - each day to the full,
Till end of life so sad the lull.
Now in Heaven, end all the pain
One never knows - life may begin again.

Elizabeth Lee

Balli Grim

While travelling through Ireland
Really deep within,
I came upon an eerie village
A place called Balli Grim.
There is no school or pub
And even the folks are grim,
There is no welcome here
At this place called Balli Grim.
It's no use trying to win them round
To smile, here is a sin.
You could be on dodgy ground
So please no lingering.
Use common sense, and please avoid,
This place called Balli Grim.

N Stokes

The Key Of 2009

Today you received the key of the door,
You have never been twenty-one before.
You mind has been finely tuned,
Your body has grown and reached full bloom.
The technology you have is worldwide,
This you have taken in your stride.
Your dreams have been put on hold
There are no jobs we are told.
Your mobile phone is your friend
You will always defend.
Houses they are plenty
But your pockets they are empty
Jobs are for the very few
So you must join the dole queue.
The Americans are debating their health care musts
Why don't they do like us and give their taxes to the trusts?
France and Germany are riding the waves
While Britain still boasts we will never be slaves.
But don't take me serious with this little verse
There are a lot more countries that are a hell of a lot worse.
I know I will always be proud of my birth
For to be born an Englishman you will always be there
To help right the wrongs in the government's snares.

Anita Quin

Ethnic Cleansing

It's too late to lock the gate,
Far too late to emigrate,
No longer can we trust to fate,
In ethnic cleansing time.

It's too late to read the news,
Someone's already lit the fuse.
No time at all to choose a pill,
Fierce fires are racing down the hill.

It's too late to abdicate,
Far too late to choose a mate.
But lots of time to kill and hate,
In ethnic cleansing time.

It's too late to compromise,
With little chance to nail the lies.
Mortar shells light up the skies,
In ethnic cleansing time.

It's too late to put down roots,
We hear the tramp of army boots
Our neighbours just can't wait to shoot,
In ethnic cleansing time.

M V Bayes

Blonde Ambition

I want to be a WAG I do.
I want to be a WAG!
To go to all the dodgy clubs
And dance around my bag.

I drink too much and smoke too much
And wear revealing clothes.
Just for kicks I often put
The white stuff up my nose.

My good points are my silicone boobs.
My talon-like scarlet nails.
With fake tan and blonde extensions,
I attract all the males.

To bag a footballer is my own goal
When I am on the lash.
His looks are not my main concern
As long as he has cash.

I would never have to work again.
I could spend every day shopping.
And when he plays away
I could always go bed-hopping.

If things did not work out
I would still have my story to sell.
We all know the newspapers
Can't resist a kiss-and-tell.

Adrianne Jones

Whispers

I stop beneath a tree and press my face to its side,
A message echoes to me, from way down deep inside,
Welcome friend, I feel the love your bringing here today,
Oh nature's child, your heart has found, a place for it to stay.
I whisper - I hear you breathing.

I sit upon the grass and close my eyes, the more to hear,
A bird is singing high above, its message rings out, loud and clear,
Dappled sunlight through the trees, strands of hair, blown by the breeze,
Nature, lets me know she's there,
I whisper - I hear you sighing.

I hear the footfall of the wildlife gathering in their way,
I know they're glad I came to call, my company they seek today,
The nearby waters trickle, passing over stony ground,
Elixir of eternal life, for living creatures, all around,
I whisper - I feel your presence, I taste your goodness.

In a forest far away, my soul's desire walks on alone,
But I'm beside him in my mind, and share the oneness all around,
Our hearts together beat as one, as our journey takes us on,
My presence felt in all he sees, in nature's garden, 'neath the trees,
With eyes closed as soft winds play, my love will hear, the words I say -

Heart of my heart, soul of my soul, breath of my breath, I'm here,
Spirit of my spirit, life of my life, I'll always hold you near,
I whisper, - renaissance man with amazing eyes, my one true love, -
I love you.

Carole Pearson

Leola

(Dedicated to James Prosser on the birth of our daughter, Leola)

On the twenty-fourth of July
Two thousand and nine
My heart started beating a wonderful chime
It happened at fourteen past three
Here on Earth for the world to see
Weighing six pounds fifteen
'A daughter!' you exclaimed to me
Tears of joy at the sound of her cry
I didn't care that she wasn't a boy
Nine months of moodiness and going through Hell
I knew by your face it was worth it, I really could tell
Tiny little fingers, tiny little toes
Tiny ear and a tiny button nose
There she was looking so very adorably sweet
Leola Lea Prosser, for us to keep.

Michelle Barnes

Harry Patch

Last man standing Harry Patch
Leave the door upon the latch
The trenches of the First World War
Will live with us for evermore
Last man standing Harry Patch
You survived the war without a scratch
Thick clinging mud was everywhere
Machine guns rattled comrades dead
Last man standing Harry Patch
Today you read your last dispatch
Barbed wire fences trapped the dead
Shells exploded overhead
Last man standing Harry Patch
Leave the door upon the latch.

David M Walford

Smart Dress Only

'Smart dress only,'
Wos wot they said.
'Let's show some respect
Fer dear ole Fred.

No sloppy jeans
Or trainer shoes
No scruffy shirt
All 'angin' loose.

Clean yer nails
An' comb yer 'air,
There's bound ter be
Relations there.

Don't bring beer
In bottles or cans,
It ain't a weddin'
Nor is it the banns!

Bring an 'anky
Ter blow yer nose,
Or 'ave yer forgotten
Ow ter use those?'

'But,' I arsked meself,
'Just wot's the sense
If me clothes ain't comfy,
An' I feel all tense?

I ain't bin
In a church before,
An I 'avent a clue
Just wot's the score.

An' does it really matter
Wot is worn,
Or if we're naked
As we were born?'

If we goes in yeller
Green, or red,
Well - Fred won't mid,
Not now 'es dead!'

Florence Barnard

Path To Success

Is it a dream or a
reflection of fantasy
that stirs in our soul
inciting desire to embrace
and turn our dream to reality
To walk the path of doubt
and prove our capabilities to achieve.

With relentless pursuit
we strive to perform
Be it not to perfection
but proud of success
whether big or small.
As faltered steps decline
self confidence will reign
enriched with desire
to reach our goal.

The reward is success
to be shared by all
proving that dreams
need not lie,
but released from the soul
by want and desire
Through toil, dedication,
and the will to succeed.

Joan Hosker

Barr Beacon

'When beeches drip in browns and duns, and thresh, and ply.
(Thomas Hardy, 'Weather')
This land only slowly yields its secret;
Barr is for Celtic for summit or top,
Pat of a ridge form Shire Oak to Queslett,
Near 750 feet above sea level reaches;
Beacon indicates that it was the spot
Where from the Druids watchfireflames
Gave notice of heathen sacrifices.
Used also by the Saxons and Danes
As a high danger alarm signal-point.

Staffordshire's and Warwickshire's choices
As their 1918 Memorial to Peace,
This windy height, long capped with beeches
Reveals widest hill and dale prospects,
Relieved by farmlands, woods and water,
Tower blocks, pylons, chimneys and churches.
All around, the lofty eminence's aspects
Command extensive wide open views.

The eye ranges far, from Dudley Castle
To Lichfield's three spires, other side takes in
All from Birmingham Town Hall, urban or rural
Almost to Wales, as far west as Wrekin,
Scenic, historical, memorable Barr Beacon.

David Daymond

In Praise Of Nature

The heady perfume
Of flowers in bloom,
The sweet smell
Of newly mown grass,
The earthy smell
Of freshly turned soil,
The sweat on your brow
At the end of a day's toil.

The sun's rays beating
Down on your back,
Cabbage whites fluttering
Above your head,
Invigorating your senses
At one with the land,
Laid out before you
By God's own hand.

Anne Williams

Salaam Means Peace

Peace in the heart
Peace of mind
Peace for the rich
Peace for the poor
Peace for big and
Peace for small
Above all
Peace for all.

Bushra Latif

Memories, Dreams And My Tears

A little child playing on cobbled streets
Precious stones collected were gems to keep
Dandelions in jam jars handpicked with care
Rags that made ringlets to pretty my hair

Dreams are the hopes that carry me through
Far away holidays by waters of blue
Castles built on golden sands
Cornfields swaying by acres of green
The shrill of birdsong to welcome the morn

Grief and its sadness appears before dawn
Black clouds float across skies of grey
My beloved son has passed away
My daughter's eyes so red and raw
Our hearts are broken for evermore

Not aware of the cruelty of life
When Frank asked me to be his wife
He promised me roses all the way
My tears replaced them from that day.

Mary Farrelly

Untitled

So you have reached age twenty-one
Don't worry that is still quite nifty
Keep providing your readers with what they enjoy
And you will still be around at fifty!

Constance Finn

Regrets

The path winds uncertainly ahead, cold grey
stones of uncertainty
which direction to take?
So many regrets, which path to bury them
in the mists of obscurity?
Years blur the edges of harsh reality, still memories come to haunt
in the black interminable night
Shadowy forms point dead fingers
mocking, taunting
The mind plays a fickle game, illusion becomes reality,
reality, illusion
Will Time cast her kindly cloak, eclipsing all self-reproach
or the years still carry doubts into infinity?
Will morning come - sunlight brilliant and unbounded
her golden rays expurgating the past
Clasping me in a compassionate embrace of forgiveness
enfolding me in her comforting arms?
Will the way then become clear and undisturbed
disquiet become tranquillity?

Merle Sadler

Goddess

On the beach we run along the sand
We jump into the sea and you bathe my soul in the waters of our love
You're sensational, for you are so irresistible and captivating
Your beauty is magnificent for you are ravishing
Looking into your angel eyes is like looking in the sea of love
Your smile could light up a city, you are mesmerising
Your beauty is hypnotic for you are like paradise
Our love will blossom like the flowers in spring
For you are everything I ever wanted
Everything I ever needed, you complete me.

Oliver Carlin

A Walk Through The Forest

I can sense that You're there Lord
I can sense that You're there.
In the fragrance of the pine trees,
And the crispness of the air.

The people walking arm in arm,
The colours of the sky.

The way the sun rests softly
On the branches of the tree,
It warms my heart to You oh Lord
And brings a smile to me.

Again, You're in a blade of grass,
In the statement that it makes
And in the flight of ducks and birds
Across the ripples of the lakes.

David Sawyer

Days Of Youth

The days of your youth will fly by,
The laughter, the good times will seem like a dream gone by,
The loves of your life will come and go,
They will become fleeting thoughts of long ago,
Your love's laughter will echo in your mind,
Do remember the good times
But remember the seasons will change,
With laughter will come the pain.
So work hard so you can succeed in all that you do,
Then one day you can fondly say, 'Long ago I was a young man too.'

Sana Arshad

Your Brain

Your brain is much more clever than today's computer,
From childhood to old age, it is recorded in there.
Your thoughts, deeds, memory are all on key to tap
Sorrows, joy, every little thing, the colour of a wasp's wing.
Dreams so vivid to recall, like opening a book, page after page,
You remember old friends, old places.
Have you ever thought what a computer can do?
Compared with your brain, imagination like animation,
It cannot be wiped out, just think of that, it is all yours,
Tap that key to your brain, it is like looking through an open door
And it is all yours, yours alone, you have only to think of a flower.
The colour and your memory keep flooding back,
A rose, a lily, a picture you have seen, it is all there.
A colour in bird's eyes, the feather on a bird's wing, you can recall,
Page after page is stamped there,
Your hurts, your love, they are yours and yours alone
Till the end of your time.

Gwen Jones

My Canine Friend

Sophie, why did you have to leave me, why did you have to go?
I loved you all these years, though sometimes it didn't show.
You came to me when I needed, and I know you felt that way too,
You turned my darkest grey skies into sunlit skies of blue.
I was there when e'er you needed but today I let you down,
I let you go without me, to dwell in a Heavenly town.
Of all the things I've known, some bad and some true,
There's none I know so faithful, so beautiful as you.
And now you sleep forever in a land of dreams
Remembering how you played with me in the rippling streams.
And walked together in the woods, chasing squirrels in the trees
And on the sandy beaches driving waves back in the seas.
These times for me are not just dreams, they are reality,
Yes, they're part of our lives together, simply parts of you and me.
So now I say goodbye to you, not for always may I say,
We both know too well we'll meet again, and together, forever stay.

George White

Oh No Romeo

Oh Romeo you stand beneath my window
Singing songs of love to win my heart,
Whilst I am sitting comfy in my armchair
Waiting for my favourite soap to start.
Though I felt flattered when you first came calling
And even Ted next door managed a smile,
We've both grown tired of your constant racket
Your choice of music's simply not our style.
I hope you'll not be out there too much longer
My boyfriend's coming soon to take me out,
He'll not take kindly to your serenading,
He'll give you something else to sing about.
But wait a moment who did you just mention?
With flowing tresses almost to her feet.
You've got it wrong dear, my name's Julianna,
Your Juliet lives further down the street!

Barbara Parker

The Fatality Of War

What is the point of going to war?
Friend and foe dying side by side
And where are those who proposed to war?
At home, living high life, full of pride.

You cannot replace one young life
Just one bullet ends the day
What a terrible thing power is
Is there no other way?

Whatever happened to live and let live
To pray, believe in peace?
Justice and a better world
Where anger and hatred cease.

There's no thought for women, children
It's men that start the wars
The women are left to pick up the pieces
And hope that peace is restored.

Sheila Hodgkins

Doorstep Salesmen

What a thankless task it must be
To try to sell goods on the doorstep to me.
Sometimes I listen, and patiently stand,
As some person goes all through their spiel.
But mostly I say, 'I don't need any today,'
You see it depends how I feel.

On the estate where I live, they all come,
From photos of kiddies, to perfumes for Mum.
I've had, double-glazing or we'll turf your lawn,
But mostly I say, 'I don't need any today,'
You see it depends how I feel.

There are the weak moments, when I do get the urge,
And perhaps, on a few brushes I'll splurge.
Sometimes for the blind or another good cause
But from countless others, no matter how hard they appeal,
I usually.say, 'I don't need any today.'
You see, it depends how I feel.

Sheila Bates

Poor People's Dream

Perhaps tomorrow will be different
Only our dreams keep us going
Obeying the rules, doing life's bidding
Rational we try and think things out

Pelf seems so far away
Energy sapped in every way
Opulence we wish would come our way
Perhaps tomorrow will be different
Luck be ours as we sleep and dream
Expecting that life could somehow seem
Suddenly different with each dream

Dear is our faith and our hope
Reaching out and doing our best
Enduring life with each difficult task
Answering each and every quest
Maybe tomorrow will be different.

Brenda Brownhill

Autumn Passes

Crimson autumn sunsets . . . mists of the morn
Dapples the stubble of harvested corn.
Vociferous seagulls follow the plough,
Ripe fruit and berries adorn every bough.
Earth yielding manna to nourish and fill,
Providing protection against winter's chill.

The September sunshine sets all too soon
Casting its rays on the October moon,
Bestowing an aura to scenes at night
Like morning's ethereal dawning light.
Fast fading roses . . . a scent we know well,
Wanes 'neath the harsher chrysanthemum smell.

O'er mountain and moorland and rolling would
Sharp autumn frosts turn the leaves to gold.
Coppery bracken in each woodland ride
Provides a haven for creatures to hide
And settle for winter - to hibernate,
Their hearts slowing down to a gentler rate.

The strenuous work of harvest is past,
The tempo of living is now less fast;
For flora and fauna have multiplied
And many a lovers knot has been tied.
But, the air is cooler . . . it's time to rest,
As autumn gives way to winter's behest.

Eric Wilks

Voices

I'm hearing voices inside my head!
These happen when it's time for me
To go to bed;
One tells me I'll never make it in this country,
Whilst another says I can quite easily.

Friend, you might be wasting time -
By pursuing a further or higher education;
For, many a rich and successful men,
Didn't attend university or college.
All you need is an idea that's sure to sell;
And, just in case your business falls through,
Don't forget that you have prayer, family,
And good friends to console you.
So, don't consider other ways, that some -
May say can be of greater help to you;
For narcotics and alcohol will only kill,
Or stupefy you.

'I'm here to make sure that you do get through,'
A third voice said in a subtle way.
'Don't make a move before you can consult me,
For you've been making too many mistakes lately.'

Tomorrow, we'll stay at home and prepare you a résumé,
The next day, go in search of employment!
Whom do you believe is stretching a hand -
To help you?
Do you say that I'm God, an idealistic figment of your imagination,
Insanity, or, am I Satan?

Osgood Browne

A Proud Nana

I am a very proud nana
For everyone to see
I have two lovely granddchildren
Who are really special to me
Kirsty is my grandaughter
Jayden is my grandson
Precious times we spend together
Having lots of fun
We do all sorts of things
Like playing in the park
I push them on the swings of course
And rock the rocking horse
To catch them giggling down the slide
Gives me such emotion that fills up inside
Two smiley faces looking innocently
Brightens my day just perfectly
As I walk with a child on either side
Two little hands firmly clutching in mine
The happiness they give me is too hard to hide
So I thank these two children who fill me with pride.

Jacqui Boote

Memories

When I was a young girl
My mother used to say
'You haven't a care in the world
Just go out to play'
I wanted to be grown up
Wear lipstick and high heels
A teenage, wife and mother
I have been
Gaining wisdom every day
Now a pensioner with hair so grey
Dear Mother long gone
How I wish I could go out to play.

Margaret Jones

Thinking With Reasoning

'Of fatherly advice' . . . Dad
I have no need in the future
I have the ability to think for myself
I now have a wife who will share in my life
We can make future decision ourself

Many a fine dream . . .'Son' . . . has been shattered
When the awakening has been premature
And so may it be in a life that is shared
Only the testing with time is one sure

'A linking in harmony' is truly a gift
Like a bird when it accompanies a song
Such are . . . two parts . . . that must work together
They are akin to that bird and its song

Thinking needs *reasoning* - they're not both the same
But each in its way plays its part
Good *'thinking with reasoning'*
Adds dimensions with meaning
Without each; they are both worlds apart

Now look far ahead . . . to that dense morning mist
'At this moment, you see nothing' . . . my son
Wait for awhile . . . just let that mist clear . . .
You'll see much further . . . to the *rise of the sun*

Enhance your *thinking* with a touch of good reasoning
Then blend both together as one
Go out into the world - there is much to be learned
It is there you will gain knowledge . . . my son

Precious metals become all the more precious
When fine workings have shown off their art
So too is life when you make right decisions
If the thinking is correct from the start

The watchmaker will fashion two components
Both must work together as one
Such knowledge should be a prize of possession
These thoughts I now pass to you . . . Son.

R L Bennett

The Blitz

My home scattered in the rubble,
Lost, scared, confused.
Fire engines parading the streets,
Worried, down-hearted, sadness.
A tear rolling down my cheek.
Miserable, unhappy, sad.
Children crying everywhere,
Left, unwanted, not cared for.
Bricks unstable,
Not safe, dangerous, devastating.
And yet the birds whistle their sweet tune
Through a bad moment of time.
The smoke makes old survivors cough
As the firemen calm the roads.
People stand devastated at the damage that has been done,
Childrens silence with terror in their little eyes,
Women; men, families, left homeless.
Sadness drowning the people in the streets
Everyone who has lost their homes gazing wide-mouthed at the rubble.
A boy hugs himself round his mother like an octopus.
The siren wails
Everybody rushes to the air raid shelters.
'Will it ever stop?' they all cry.

Priya-Jasmine Sangha

Word Picture

Green fields are freckled with a golden sheen
Of buttercups, and on the still warm air
There hangs the hawthorn hedge's sweet perfume;
Far off the cuckoo calls, and everywhere
The green-massed trees are vivid in new leaf;
And in their shade lie cattle, velvet-eyed,
Chewing away their lives in quiet content,
And here a mare is grazing, at her side
A slender long-legged foal; horse-chestnut trees
Display their flower candles, pink and white
And drop confetti petals on the ground;
And every cottage garden now is bright
With fragrant wallflowers: the laburnums toss
Their golden tassels at the lilac plumes
And glow against the dusky copper-beech
Like galaxies among celestial glooms.
And in the woods, beneath the sun-laced trees
A mist of bluebells and a choir of birds;
I never saw a day so exquisite!
How can one show such loveliness in words?

Eileen Bales

The Future

The future is tomorrow,
and the day that's yet to pass,
a moment, from a moment,
the hour in a glass,
a minute from a minute
the seconds in next week,
the warmth of summers yet to come, and winters that are bleak.

The future is a new day
where dreams for some come true,
for some there's disappointment,
for all it's something new,
where fates have been decided,
and we don't really know,
but only time will tell us,
so onward we must go.

The future is predictions,
the plans so full of hope,
where people who are affluent,
see poor ones left to cope,
and there we will be older,
and some will be more wise,
and some will live in honesty,
opposing people's lives.

Go forward to your future,
for you I hope it's fine,
you'll be there in one moment,
or when you've read this line.

Trevor Wiggan

Handbag

She holds the tiny clasp between forefinger and thumb, pushes gently.
Small particles of dust fall like mist upon her sleeve.

Her hand shades her eyes. She squints in to the dark interior.
The scent of sickly sweet toffee merges with the slightest whiff of peppermint.
Hidden in the dark damask, a diminutive pair of silvery keys.

Keys that can chart her heart. Open her mind to forgotten occurrences.
Jealousies, growing pains of adolescence, hurtful silences.
All written down with a careful hand. A covert diary of her youth.

First day at the factory. Stark white overalls, matching mob hat.
Fashion and style quashed for eight long hours.
Two young girls with steely bright eyes whisper and snigger,
Point and giggle, waiting to swoop.

Her demeanour is one of innocence, her nails are sugary pink.
Bedraggled strands of auburn hair escape from beneath her cap.
Never acknowledging their presence or meeting their piercing gaze,
But alone with her diary, they are captured in inky black writing,
Black as soot.

She holds the keys tightly clenched inside her palm,
Remembering her tormentors who plagued and teased,
Diminishing her confidence. Trying to remain in the shadows,
Not be part of their prey.

Her eyes adjust to the gloom of the attic.
Deep in the nucleus of the house she catches a fragment of conversation.
The shy retiring girl is no longer evident,
She is tall and willowy, has confidence and grace.
The handbag now closed, forgotten,
An empty husk of another life.

Heather Lynes-King

Man On Wire

(Philippe Petit's celebrated wire walk between the Twin Towers on 7th August, 1974)

It's a new day and eyes are drawn from grey
Pavements, from the dead-ahead up, up,
Sky-high. Can you see? It takes time to focus

Then jaws drop in disbelief. A night-spun thread
Linking the fated Towers and a man's out there
In the impossible between. It roots us

To the spot. The giddy Twins are racing
The clouds while he takes his ease on his
One-inch wire reclines in turbulent mid-air

As in a garden hammock caressed
By the lightest breeze. Now he kneels, stands,
Pirouettes; a dance of life at its utmost edge,

Spirit in its freest element of focussed
Mastery. He's called to come down but he won't.
Each small steady step's a giant leap

Of spirit that sends all the broken regulations
Tumbling, pitched to scatter on the early
Morning air in glorious confusion.

It's the stuff of legend, a wire walk
To the brink of ourselves, arresting
The Dead-Ahead with a cleaving shaft

Of the Vertical.

David Donaldson

October Mist

October is mist creeping in and around,
Hiding the houses, deadening the sound:
Playing its tricks on the mind and the eye,
Enfolding, embracing, then floating on high
The chimney tops, aerials, whose periscope spires
Reach on, ever upward, higher and higher,
Unanchored and ghostly, eerily free,
Sailing in limbo, adrift on white sea.

The waves twist and swirl, then slowly withdraw,
Creeping on downwards to play nearer the floor,
To torment and tantalise, touch and to tease,
Making ogres and spectres of bushes and trees.
The fingers of fog slide through autumn-tinged leaves,
And the branches drop tears as they hauntingly wheeze.
Gauze webs are transformed by mist's magical hands,
Hanging diamonds and dewdrops on all of their strands.

When it tires of tame mischief and glittering jewels,
Mist changes its mood to tauntingly cruel.
It drifts, first thinly, then thick as a wall,
Making vision impossible, no sight at all,
It entices and beckons to challenge Man's pride
To pierce through and conquer - but hidden inside
That writhing white shroud of wraithlike breath,
In blood and burnt wreckage is the spectre of Death.

Betty Tordoff

Adlestrop Revisited

The trains no longer stop
At Adlestrop -
The station done away with years ago;
And where the platform used to be
Grow now willow-herb and grass -
Luxuriantly.

No haycocks either dry
Beneath a June sky:
Now huge cylindrical bales, bound and sheeted,
Cast packaged shadows over prairie meadows.
Birdsong once filled these acres - when
Birds had hedgerows.

Yes, Adlestrop, the name -
Only the name
That strikes a mournful note within this heart:
With everything weighed - the profit and cost
The intervening years have wrought -
I could not but reflect on something
Precious lost.

Philip Sanders

Grandma's Expertise

'I'm amazed that you can do such a thing,' he said,
'Especially when you're lying on the bed.'
'Oh, it's easy,' I replied, 'You just do that, and then this.'
'Good heavens,' said he, 'I'd give that a miss.'
'Does it mean you're' double joined, and very fit?'
'Not really, everyone in my family does it.'
'Just like that, in that sort of way?'
'Oh my grandma does it better, I'm glad to say,
She can twist it like this, and push it up there,
Believe me, that causes the family to stare,
But there again, it takes a lifetime, to do it well,
And she's expert, I grant you, a real pro, my old gel.'

Peter Corne

Stargazer

One night I sailed far out to sea beyond the loom of earthly light
And looking upward saw the stars like twinkling crystals shining bright
Each little sparkling speck a sun, set in the vast celestial sphere
Of reachless space and endless time so far away and so yet clear
And as I gazed it came to me that without stars what would we be?
Alone in space nowhere, no place, beyond this world eternity
Of black oblivion, nothing there, a void, a chaos without sense
No stars or worlds beyond our own, just empty space, no evidence
Of order, meaning, celestial power, of cosmic purpose, guardian hand
Aware of us small though we are, less than the smallest grains of sand
Amongst the vastnesses of space, the lonely, wondering human race
Lives on and dreams upon the stars, its future resting on the grace
Of architect that fashioned all, from atom size to mighty suns
Created life both great and small from tiny ants to pachyderms
O let the stars shine forth each night to give us hope that out in space
There's hope, a future for our race.

G White

Heavenly Dance

The music entranced me as I stepped from my body.
As easily as slipping out of a worn out gown.
I threw back my head and laughed with excitement,
As my spirit was lifted, my feet took flight.
A garland of flowers was placed on my head,
Gone were the grey, lustreless locks.
Instead, long curls, shimmering, shining, swirling around in the heavenly dance.
My limbs did not ache, they were agile and nubile.
The gown that I wore was as light as the air.
The music played on, oh how I danced in its merry throng.
All was beauty of many colours, hills and trees of emerald green.
I threw back my head and laughed with sheer joy.
Pain had gone and with it all sorrows.
This picture is all I have, I could see no further.
Back in my body for a while longer I must be.
But the memory I have of the beautiful music and the hope that one day I will dance and be free.

Margaret Ashfield

A Breath Of Spring

Outside the golden daffodils are dancing in the breeze,
Their faces turned towards the sun.
They edge the fresh green carpet,
Waiting to herald all who walk upon.

The apple and the pear tree stand sentinel each side,
Their branches held out to the sun,
Patiently waiting to burst their buds,
And so dress themselves in green.

A willow stands there proudly,
Her blossom in full bloom.
Soon she will lose her first spring coat
And adorn herself in green.

The speckled thrush completed the scene,
A tasty morsel he hopes to find,
While a blackbird in a tree nearby
Sings to the world its own sweet song.

Christine Preece

Merry Miser

I qualified as a medical man
ideal to start a savings plan.

'Twas private fees not the National Health
that made me smile and start my wealth.

A good bedside manner attracts the pound
my till ringing merrily is a wonderful sound.

I'm left mountainous sums from patients gone southerly
look sombre to widows and let them act motherly.

What shall I do with my overstocked hoard?
Can't let it be known how much it has soared.

At three score and ten, I'll spend some for sure
But not at the moment, I abhorred being poor.

A Rice

Hands In The Country

The cuckoo has flown, he calls no more,
They are scarce now, not many visit our shore.
The blackberry season is upon us again,
Beautiful fruit because of the rain.
This means blackberry and apple jam and pie,
Blackberries picked from brambles on high.
Not many brambles are left to grow either,
They are thorny, straggly, untidy - a hazard.
Whole orchards of plums have gone under the disc
Pick your own used to be fun, now it is pick your own at your own risk.
You might slip on a plum and fall flat on your bum
Then the grower must pay a hefty sum!
Treat the black pear tree in Worcester with fear and dread,
One of these pears could kill you stone dead!
Don't laugh it's not funny, injuries could cost the council money.
A pear? You might ask, you are taking the Mick,
Oh no! These pears are deemed dangerous,
They are behind bars in their own nick.

Jeanette Middleton

The Gift Of Thought

Like a dawn retreating, the sunset gleams, leaving a residue of Turner sky,
Gold on white with deeper blues being chased by a gathering grey.

The passing day nears its time to rest, with darkness, a pillow to lay on.
Leaving time to ponder, collect one's thoughts, or a carpet of dreams to fly on.

Turn off the world, become just one, immune to the intrusion of any other,
Seek sanctuary and freedom through space of thought, in the comforting arms of slumber.

For the speed of light is but a worm, when imagination soars in wonder,
As the mind of Man is a priceless gift, when compared to acquisitive plunder.

Nurture your gift of thought and reason; enjoy its borders far-reaching,
Be not a mere beast in nature's field, for without our minds, we amount to nothing.

Graham Griffiths

Old Photographs

The echoes of a distant time
Of work done long ago
Of triumphs and of tragedies
Of pleasure and of woe.

Old pictures of our ancestors
Of folk we've never known
In streets we walk in still today
Streets thought of as our own.

Of factory buildings long pulled down
Their fires have long gone cold
Their anvils silenced one by one
Their stories never told.

Families standing in the yard
The children all at play
The washing hanging on the line
The sky a misty grey.

The schoolroom shots, the public house
The charabanc outside
The chapel outings in the spring
To the country, just a ride.

Those moments frozen for all time
On celluloid or glass
A memory we can live again
A memory just, alas.

Ron Smith

Insomnia

The snorer and the nightingale
are singing in my head.
The nightingale, a branch away;
my husband, in my bed.

And while I love the nightingale's
distinctive warbling song,
I sometimes wish the wretched bird
would carol on less long!

My husband's no percussionist,
nor side-drum, tymps, nor snare;
stentorian, he trumpets on
with little gasps for air.

I sing for all insomniacs;
my tribute paid in hours.
To think men claim that birdsong vies
with Heaven's celestial choirs!

And when, at length, the nightingale is mute;
why, oh for scorn;
the cuckoo and the collared dove
salute the early dawn!

John Burman

Fantasy

In the dark stillness of night,
When the peace of slumber evades me,
Thoughts take over my wandering mind.
I'm enveloped by fantasy.

Would I travel to far distant shores?
Languish on golden sands beneath skies of blue?
Where the sun is forever shining,
Where life is different, exciting, and new.

But if this were so, would it last?
When its image had slowly passed away,
Would I yearn for that familiar life I knew
And of friends that brighten up my day?

I would miss the glistening dew upon a rose,
The perfume of honeysuckle in the air.
Friendly faces I see each day
People I love, whose company I share.

That first joyous glimpse of spring
When the long dreary winter is over.
The sweet sound of the blackbird's song,
A carpet of bluebells, enchanted with clover.

How could I leave all this behind?
These treasures I hold most dear.
Straying thoughts must remain a fantasy
For my heart tells me I belong here.

J Wicks

Noor Inayat Khan

An orchid of bewitching kind
Recurring in the sentient mind;
With gentleness that of a fawn,
A petalled image cruelly torn.

With love the rarest dreams embrace
Faith constant in her lovely face;
Cloaked service that the best might seek,
Sun breaking on a dark-capped peak.

Alone enchained, a flower blown
Against an awesome tyrants throne;
Defiant at that wall of death
She yielded up her life's young breath.

Her goodness only mocked her foes,
White, untrod, high Tibetan snows;
This daughter of a royal line
Now woven into God's design.

And liberté her final word
At Dachau said for what occurred;
A brass-set plaque, soul-shivered time,
Revered as many prayers sublime.

Christopher Rothery

Imagine

I wake to a lonely, empty room,
I sometimes wake in the night,
I imagine for just a few moments,
and then I turn on the light.

I imagine I'm singing and laughing,
just like my life before,
I think I can even hear you,
turning your key in the door.

I'd like to do something useful
but those days seem long in the past,
I thought I had what I wanted,
but I thought and it didn't last!
I thought I'd turned the corner on a long and winding road,
but instead my back was hurting, and I couldn't carry the load.

I'd like for just a few moments
to stop the world going round.
I'd like to go back to the beginning
and hold onto that something I found.

June Sedgebear

Holding On

(Dedicated to my husband Simon)

Time's gone by and here we are,
You're my ray of light, my guiding star.
I love you more than I've ever done,
After having our daughter and then our son.
Sleepless night and tensions run high,
Our love may be gifted but I still cry.
Things will be normal again some day,
Back on our path we'll find our way.
I kiss your lips and memories are there,
I touch your face, I feel your stare.
I long for you to hold me again,
You're deep in my heart, I feel no pain.
When your arms surround me, I'm lost in space,
You take me to another world, a different place.
Guided by you, I'm yours to take,
This is for keeps I will not forsake.
I hope that one day, when we have wrinkles to show,
That I have proved my love, only you will know.
So here's to the future and whatever it may hold,
This is forever until we are old.

Kerry Lovatt

Digital TV

I remember TV as it used to be, black and white, BBC1, ITV, '62
BBC2, colour came too, '82 Channel Four. Turned left to right,
BBC1 30 left, BBC2 31 right, ITV 32 left, Channel Four 33 right.

'95 Channel Five, breezed through 'Brainteaser' now digital age comes ablaze
ITV2, 3,4, even More Four, shopping at store
QVC, Bid TV, Ideal World, BBC News 24/7, this is Heaven and BBC Radio 7.

TV's a con, yesterday's gone, goodbye analogue,
TV comes of age with raised eyes.
Choice of channels across the globe to USA,
Government spend millions, billions, 72 TV, 23 radio, 95 in all and it's your call.

Digital age is upon us is a rage, lost in a maze.
This is TV but not as we know it, if it were a boat, we'd row it,
Out goes the old in comes bold.

In 2011 we switch over, we'll be in clover. TV got wise, analogue goes bye-byes
Sizes from 32-100 inch, fit in with a pinch.
Licences rocket, burn holes in pockets, don't knock it, plug in socket,
Flick through channels, these days, we sit in chairs and zap them with remotes.

Michael Thomas Hill

November Fun

The evening is misty, smell smoke in the air
Pets hide in the house under a bed or chair
A bonfire's glow lights up the sky
Soon the flames will reach the guy
Little fingers holding sparklers
Little hands warmed by the fire
The sound of children's laughter, they will not tire
Fountains of pretty stars listen to the *ooos* and *aahs*
Bangers with a very loud sound jumping jacks chase one around
Rockets zooming up to Mars
Bake potato and burger bars
Warm in anoraks and wellies
It makes a change from the telly.
This is a night to remember
Fun in the park on the 5th of November.

J Brown

Henry Died Aged 113 (1896-2009), Harry Died Aged 111 (1898-2009)

Henry Allingham aged 113,
Harry Patch aged 111,
It's not their longevity that defines them,
These two brave heroes of the Great War
The War to end all wars!

It's in their strength of character,
That tightly closed door within the sub-conscious,
They begin to share those harrowing experiences,
Hoping their message will never be forgotten.

We owe our survival to all who fought for us,
Forever in their gratitude,
Therefore it's our duty to use the oxygen we breathe to survive,
To fuel that truth to speak out,
Ensuring future generations understand the futility of war.

Why dictators?
Why greed?
Why control?

We are all Earthlings,
On borrowed time,
To share this planet and space.

To tolerate!
To love!
To try!

It sounds like a dream,
But maybe dreams can come true!
Peace, love,
It's all we really have!

Please, please don't waste it,
Use it wisely,
We can live in hope,
Just like Henry and Harry.

Marilyn Simper

Sea Swans At West Shore

I caught this Easter morning
six stately swans -
still on the water,
serene in the sun - bright,
crisp April air
and for their backcloth Mother Snowdon
and her purple brood
resplendent.

As morning passed the drone
on shore grew apace
but they went heedless
of the dogs barking
and children shouting
as they ran
and played where once
young Miss Liddell played.

Throughout the day they remained,
occasionally to forage in the shallows
but mostly to ride the glassy
Conwy waters
all with an air of disdain
staking their claim
to this special place,
this hallowed piece of Cymru.

When the crowds are gone
I will come again
and stand
in hope of reprise

but at a distance.

Dave K Whalley

Dream Lover Or Perchance To Dream

As shades of night fall
Veils of mystery spread
Faded memories recall
Bright glints in shimmering thread

From golden hours spun
Brushing the air with dreams
On hushed footstep you come
Down glittering moonbeams.

Tender is the night
The warmth your love brings
Stealing softly around me
Now my heart sings

Delighting in every moment
Memories captured to hold
Happiness printed on rich cloth
Edged in precious gold

Heaven's blue has dimmed her stars
Pale moonlight flickers, adieu
Only echoes now, whispering darling,
My darling, I love you, love you.

Joan Hawkes

Nameless

When she first started acting oddly,
I could have called her Twit-Face.
And as she became more ungodly,
Maybe even Nit-Face.
But since she's sailed through our life,
A destroyer bringing strife,
I've decided to settle for Ship-Face.

Judy Barklam

Let Sleeping Dogs Lie

What do you do when you love someone so much that it hurts to be near them
Do you let them know, so you can talk about it
Or do you try to let go and try to forget
The times that love was shared?

What do you do when every day you find your thoughts are with them
When at the same moment in time
You're wishing all these thoughts would go away?
They won't, they just keep on getting stronger.

What do you do when you keep on trying to convince yourself
That this love has nowhere to go
Or is it that your real fear
Is its intensity and its openness?

What do you do when you know that
This is the love you've been searching, all through your life for?
Yet for circumstances far beyond your control
This love may never be allowed to be.

What do you do with the aching heart
The tears that fall, then dry?
With the love that grows and despairs, because in your soul
You know that you may never love this way again?

What do you do when the part of you that has never allowed
Itself to be touched, has been touched for the very first time?
When although you now feel vulnerable deep down inside
You want to give your all and not your nothing.

What do you do when the spirit within you wants to unfold
To love with both its heart and soul, unconditionally?
It reaches out to touch and often feels
Another spirit's presence there, beside you.

What do you do when you don't listen to the advice you've both been given?
When minds and bodies merge to become one, if only for a short time?
When the human you've become is now afraid, yet still you love?
Will friendship alone ever be enough knowing that you both want . . . each other?

What do you do when you know that things will never be the same again?
That both your lives are about to change and take on a new meaning?
When in your confusion you're wondering why it all had to happen this way?
And you're wondering where all this is going to end.

What do you do when you want them to know that if they're willing to

Take that chance on letting you in and trusting you
You will always have that love and will always walk beside them
Even if that closeness sometimes still hurts?

What do you do when you want them to know that you'll share their experiences
Both good and bad and that their pain and fear can ease
Helping them to become one within once more?
You also want them to know, to believe
That with love, anything is possible.

Tracey Skivington

Dreams

I want chocolates, I get flowers instead.
I want strawberries, grapes I get fed.

I want to party, at home I did stay.
I want to fly, but I get grounded that day.

I want help building sandcastles, not just be given the sand.
I want things to work out, the things I have planned.

I want to walk on a moonlit beach with the waves lapping at my toes.
I want to sit by a log fire, till the flames have gone and the ember glows.

I want to hold someone's hand, looking up to the stars in the sky,
Feel the wind in my face, watch the clouds rolling by.

I want to walk in a wood, with trees all around.
Listen to the birds, their twittering sound.

I want to walk, skip, jump and run.
Be really silly, just having fun.

I want to see dolphins, swimming in the sea.
Twisting and jumping. To say hello to me.

I want to see sights, places, people and drink
Until my head's full, I can no longer think.

I want to share all, these dreams of mine
With a caring person, who has the time?

I want to love and protect them, like princes do.
Are you my princess? Do dreams come true?

Mark L Hewitt

The Lime In Autumn's Fall

Oh, mighty tree of ages you change and give and shed.
Sparse boughs bent in twisted form, asleep not dead.
Vivid the colours kissed by the morning dew,
end of evening night. The dawn, mist breaks through.
On yonder bank, the mellow willows weep a weathered sight.
Yet you, my lime, spread your branches autumn's delight.

Gently falling, spiralling, drifting down, no breeze.
Nature's force sweeps clean, you bequeath your yellow leaves
with glory, honours, nature's rich, every golden leaf.
They lie now brown, in shuffling piles over the grass beneath.

It is a privilege to watch to see your leaves blow free.
Your bark shines with a radiance, shadows, an opening key.
A power of a greater force than man, nature, paths lend new worth.
Man must understand, the power of her face on this beloved Earth.

Grace Anderson

Why Do We Still Have Wars?

Over the years we seem to have learned nothing.
We are supposed to be the superior species
Then why are we still, with other countries fighting?
Is it for a tiny bit of oil or for their land leases?
Our solders fighting and losing their lives
Mums and dads, girlfriends and boyfriends and other ties.
Wondering whether they will ever return to their homes
Why can't we have peace for every country in the world?
Why do people hate so much they have to fight?
We were put on this Earth to get along with each other
So why do we still have wars?

Zoe French

Forward Press Information

We hope you have enjoyed reading this book - and that you will continue to enjoy it in the coming years.

If you like reading and writing poetry drop us a line, or give us a call, and we'll send you a free information pack.

Alternatively if you would like to order further copies of this book or any of our other titles, then please give us a call or log onto our website at www.forwardpress.co.uk

Forward Press Information
Remus House
Coltsfoot Drive
Peterborough
PE2 9JX
(01733) 890099